# The Shalom Woman

## Margaret Wold

AUGSBURG PUBLISHING HOUSE
MINNEAPOLIS, MINNESOTA

THE SHALOM WOMAN

Copyright © 1975 Augsburg Publishing House

Library of Congress Catalog Card No. 75-2828

International Standard Book No. 0-8066-1475-7

Scripture quotations unless otherwise noted are from the Revised Standard Version of the Bible, copyright 1946, 1952, and 1971 by the Division of Christian Education of the National Council of Churches.

Manufactured in the United States of America

## The Shalom Woman

# 1

## Her Common Journey

Fog foamed in the Los Angeles International Airport when the immense jet lifted off the runway and broke through into the sunshine above the California coastline. As the plane executed its turn eastward, the fuzzy fog blanket below shrank in size exposing mountains and deserts hot and barren under the June sun.

My spirit soared with the plane as it leveled off at 37,000 feet. I was on my way to keep an appointment in West Berlin with 159 women from 49 countries around the world at a consultation whose purpose was to explore all that it means to be a woman in our world today.

Miles below us clouds were herding together again. On their white backs the sun printed the shadow of the plane and its jet trail like a giant arrow pointing toward new possibilities.

New possibilities?

West Berlin and a meeting with the somewhat overwhelming theme "Sexism in the 1970s: Discrimination

Against Women" was an unlikely destination for a woman married for three decades to the same husband, the mother of five children. Certain other labels—labels seemingly inconsistent with the meeting's purpose—might also describe me. As a Christian I suppose I might be tagged with such phrases as "born again," serious-minded," "Spirit-filled," and the many similar words descriptive of a pastor's wife and church woman in her middle years.

What could make a woman with such a description look forward so eagerly to being a participant in this global consultation with the far-out name?

Many women are taking a second look at their personal histories, examining them in the light of God's calling for each human life, and discovering a yawning abyss separating their potentials from their opportunities. I thought about those hundreds of other women I had met in my travels as a speaker and lecturer and as the executive director of a national church women's auxiliary. So many were traveling similar roads—from total acceptance of their traditional roles to a profound questioning of the limitations imposed on women as contributors to the whole of life by both society and the church.

Yet I was also painfully aware of the attempts to polarize women into "pro" and "anti" women's lib groups and of the need for reconciling voices which could address themselves to the concerns of both groups. As is frequently true in liberation movements, the voice of moderation is rarely popular and seldom heeded. Yet it is the position at which the swinging pendulum of action and reaction must find common energy if the factors which propelled it to move in the first place are ever to be dealt with constructively.

All voices need to be listened to and heard. The needs and hurts of the woman who is dependent on her own efforts for survival and support must not be taken lightly by the woman who comfortably receives her support from a caring husband. The self-sufficient professional woman cannot derogate the woman who has chosen the care of a family as her vocation. Women in lands of plenty must open their understanding to the plight of those women who live in areas where freedom from hunger or racism or economic oppression is the only liberation that concerns them.

I anticipated that this conference would provide me with opportunities for an understanding of women's concerns on a less provincial scale than I had ever experienced before.

As the jumbo jet fled from the sunset into the sunrise, I thought of Carl Jung's statement that to be a modern person is to have a conscious awareness of who one is in one's own time.[1] Jesus said it so simply in John 8:31, "If you continue in my word, you are truly my disciples, and you will know the truth, and the truth will make you free." For the Christian person, that's where conscious awareness is rooted. Modern women, in the reclaiming of their own personal histories, are moving rapidly toward the sunrise of new knowledge about who they truly are in God's church and world *in this present hour*.

The tragedy for so many is that they don't "continue" in the Word, but they are content with the small beginnings of revelation, content with small answers to small questions, and so never move on into the full awareness of the truth that completely frees.

Freedom in Christ is a journey toward wholeness, rather than a destination. The Christian enters into all that life in Christ promises in Baptism, and from that time the journey is toward understanding oneself fully, "even as I have been fully understood," because now I know only "in part" (1 Cor. 13:12). We never fully

7

arrive until our end comes, but we are constantly in process of becoming.

My own process of becoming had taken me through a master's degree in theology, through years of Bible study, through graduate courses in education, psychology, speech, and drama. It had kept me open to any of the gifts God's Spirit had for me, and it had turned me around and sent me in new directions many times. Now it had taken me into a conscious awareness, a growing conviction over a couple of decades, that something was terribly wrong with church structures which denied women opportunity to exercise freely their Spirit-given gifts and natural talents in all areas of the church's life and mission. Theology, history, and tradition had all combined with cultural conditioning to support the subjugation of women in the church.

It's true that some individual men see in the mirror of their own oppressions the inequities and the injustices perpetrated on women as clearly as some women do, and they understand as do these women that we are trapped—men and women alike—in structures which produce, promote, and perpetuate sexism. Along with growing numbers of such women and men, I had grown in my conviction that to be true to the gospel as Jesus Christ had proclaimed it (Luke 4:18) and lived it, I had to follow God's Spirit wherever that led me into human liberation.

Some years ago in the writing of my master's thesis, I had become intrigued by the whole concept of *shalom*. Choosing to make a study of the Greek word for *peace* (*eirene*) in the New Testament, I soon discovered that *eirene* could only be understood in the context of the Hebrew word *shalom*. By translating *eirene* with the one word *peace*, we have lost so much of what the Scriptures want us to understand when they speak of the fact that

8

God sent his Son as the "Prince of Shalom" (Isa. 9:6). Centuries later, Jesus personally gave his shalom as a gift to his followers with the simple statement, "My shalom I give to you" (John 14:27). Just as simply, the Apostle Paul identifies the crucified Jesus with shalom: "He is our peace" (Eph. 2:14).

How did he become our shalom? By making "us both one" through his destruction of the "dividing wall of hostility" which kept Gentiles and women separated from the worshiping congregation in separate areas of the temple. Those walls, leveled by the force of Christ's reconciling shalom, ought never to have been raised again! Persons in the church who are concerned for its health are seeking to understand the theological and historical processes which rebuilt them.

After all, "wholeness" is the primary meaning of shalom and that means that if one part of the body suffers, all suffer. So the shalom woman longs for that "wholeness" in the church which is the complete spectrum of all that ties the word "salvation" so closely to shalom. Isaiah weds the two concepts when he exclaims, "How beautiful upon the mountains are the feet of him who brings good tidings, who publishes shalom, who brings good tidings of good, who publishes salvation" (Isa. 52:7). From their use in the Scriptures, it seems that shalom, or peace, is the lasting state of salvation.

We were scheduled for an equipment change in Washington, D.C., which meant that we were to be transferred from our large, comfortable jet to a much smaller plane for the ocean crossing. I was given a middle seat between two young people, the one on my right an army M.P. returning to his post in Germany; the one on my left a Peace Corps worker who trained other young people to go to Iran. Our flight was delayed three hours, and darkness had come to the Atlantic before we took off.

9

As we followed the coastline north before heading for the open sea, I closed my eyes and wondered what those other 159 women were doing. *Are they, too, on planes and trains, hurtling across continents and seas to keep our appointment in West Berlin? Are they wondering to what that appointment will give birth? Even though they think in other languages, are their feelings about themselves similar to mine? Are their dreams tonight dreams of wholeness and shalom?*

I was to learn that prophetic female voices are rising in such disparate places as Nigeria, New Zealand, in Asia, in Central and South America, in affluent and underdeveloped countries, among rich and poor.

I was to become convinced that the awakening of women all over the world to a personal and corporate quest for wholeness was Spirit-born. There is no other way to adequately account for the universality of this phenomenon.

I had brought my tape recorder and would ask some of the women I met to share their personal stories and the stories of the women among whom they lived and were identified.

In West Berlin, Brigalia Bam had already arrived at Evangelischer Johannesstift, the evangelical community in the suburb of Spandau where the consultation was scheduled. The sturdy turn-of-the-century red brick buildings that sheltered a thousand persons—the aged, the orphaned, the mentally disturbed, the physically ill, and the forgotten—clustered around the spired building at their center. Brigalia had not slept well the night before as she mentally checked and rechecked the preparations for this most important first-of-its-kind consultation.

*I wonder what they'll look like, these women with whom I've been corresponding for over ten months. I wonder if those who live under difficult political situations have gotten their passport and visa problems taken care of. It's been fascinating to read the forms filled out in many languages in which they tell about themselves, their families, their ages, their experiences. I wonder if they're going to fit the mental pictures I've drawn of them?*

*I almost feel in awe of the training and experience these women have had. They are lawyers, magistrates, members of parliaments, university professors, and I wonder how they will feel about the consultation—if it will have been worth their leaving important jobs to spend a whole week talking with other women from around the world.*

*Have we forgotten anything? Did we remember to bring all the papers, the texts of the speeches? Would all of the translation equipment be on time?*

Brigalia forced herself to think of other things, trusting that the preparations made in the Geneva office of the World Council of Churches had been adequate and that everyone who came would have a room to sleep in, would be fed and would be stimulated by the experience.

Her mind was free then to think about another matter which had been weighing heavily on her the past few days. Her brother, 37 years old, had been a political prisoner in South Africa for the past eleven years. Six weeks earlier he had been released. As a black South African he had been cut off from life all of this time.

*What will his reaction be when he gets the letter I wrote to him this morning?* she wondered. *He's been out of touch with things for so long. Will he understand why I'm now involved in such an issue as "sexism"? He hasn't even known these years that women all over the world have grown increasingly concerned about their identity in the structures of church and society since he went to prison. I don't want him, after suffering so much because of his struggle against the terrible racism in our country, to think that I've forgotten about that oppression and have gotten caught up in some "women's lib" bandwagon. I want him to understand that what we are doing now as women is simply another part of the larger issue of the gospel and the liberation of all people from whatever evils hold them in bondage.*

In Southampton, England, young Polly Haslam was saying goodbye to her husband and children. The astonishment of the young wives living in the community served by their Methodist church was no greater over her pastor husband's willingness to stay home with two small children than it was over Polly's decision to leave them for a week in order to go alone to West Berlin! Their understanding of marriage roles did not permit such unique opportunities for either the mothers or the fathers of young children. Polly herself wrestled with certain anxieties about her journey but felt a great need to go and test some of her perceptions against those of women from other cultures.

*My whole concern with the women thing started, I think, from an awareness of how the people around us in Southampton just are not permitted to be people in the fullest sense, and that means both men and women, but it's particularly the women who are not allowed to be anything they choose to be. At least the men have some kind of choice in their job and where they spend most of their time, but as working-class wives the women very often have no choice at all.*

*I'm going to the consultation because I think it's important. I think the whole issue is important. The number of women taking tranquilizers, the number of women needing to talk but so shut up within themselves, the number of women needing to drink, is appalling. And maybe men, too—I mean certainly men, too. All this points to a great need in society especially for women. There is something which is sick, and I think the church needs to be more concerned than it is now.*

*I'm talking now about England, I can't talk about the Third World where the problems are obviously very different. We have enough to eat, but I'm not sure that we're allowed to BE as people.*

Shanti Zechariah had just been informed three days before that she had been selected to represent the Council of Churches in Malaysia at the consultation. She was not even sure how relevant the topic would be in her particular community, since the inferior status of women is so deeply entrenched in their religious thought and life that even to question it would be unthinkable for them. She knows that if she, as one of a Christian minority, told the women in her community to work for free opportunity for themselves, they would be terribly frightened to go against their own Holy Word, the Koran.

As she packed her bright saris, Shanti's black eyes sparkled under the crimson spot on her brown forehead, remembering how she had come to Malaysia in the first place.

*When you are 18 or 19 you have the world at your feet and on your shoulders and you want to do things which if you thought about them now you think how foolish you were, but sometimes it pays off. As a university student I wrote a ten-point plan for the rehabilitation of Indian prisoners of war who had been forced by the Japanese to work on the Burma Death Railway to link Burma and Malaysia through Thailand. I sent the paper to the High Commissioner of India and he wrote to ask for an appointment with me! I'll never forget that*

13

he said, "I wanted to see the girl who wrote this big memorandum to somebody like me."

So I was sent with a team to Singapore to resettle over 250,000 Indian migrants. When India and Malaysia achieved independence, I returned to help organize the Indian laborers on the large rubber plantations and now work full-time with the plantation workers' union. I married a first generation Malaysian from India and we have three children.

The slender dark-haired woman asked to be identified only as Marie.

I am Brazilian of Japanese descent. My parents immigrated to Brazil after they lost all of their belongings in Tokyo in the earthquake of 1922. Because of the overcrowding in Japan, they decided to move to Brazil where there was a need for manpower for the coffee farms. But they were not physically fit for the heavy work, and after two years my father opened a barber shop in a city and worked all his life to give proper education to his seven children. I could say that in my case, although I come from a very poor family, I am a very privileged person because any person in Brazil who can get a university education should consider herself very privileged. It is really a minority that can even complete high school education. Now I am a social worker, and my family is of the Evangelical Holiness Church.

You know many people from foreign families have the problem of knowing who they are, whether they are still foreigners or whether they belong to the country in which they live. In my case, this was very important to find my own identity. Many times people ask me whether I would like to live in Japan, and I couldn't ever consider this possibility. I belong entirely to Brazil. That's my

*home. My future, my destiny, is very strongly related to
my fellow Brazilians.*

The father of tall, gentle-voiced Tamo Diro was one
of the last New Guinean males in his area to go through
tribal initiation ceremonies; later he became a Christian
missionary with the United Church of Papua New
Guinea.

*Because my father was a missionary I went first to
the mission school where my father was the teacher.
In the 1950s we had to sit in the hot sun and write in
the sand—ABC and 1-2-3. After going to government
school, I won an administration scholarship—the only
girl in competition with 20 boys—and went to Australia
to study.*

*My own people look with suspicion on educated
women who live in European-style houses, and drive
cars; they have this image that we don't eat the same
food as they do and are very different. It took me a long
time to bridge this gap, and now I am accepted wherever
I go. I'm a community development worker.*

*You see, we're a poor country, and every year the
Australian government gives us 150 million dollars, but
half of that goes to the wages of white people because
they're paid such high salaries. The minimum average
wage in Papua New Guinea is $16 a fortnight, and a
family of six cannot survive on that, yet we are expected
to go to the same schools with people who get two and
three hundred dollars a fortnight. Women are especially
oppressed under this system because parents just won't
spend the money to send their daughters to school.*

Helen Hee-Kyung Chung, principal of a Christian high
school in Korea where 3,700 girls study, is a woman of

15

great strength of character who has a good deal of power in her church and community. After receiving a university education on a scholarship in her own country she was sent to the U.S. by her government to get graduate training. With a strong sense of loyalty to her government she agonizes over the division of her land into North and South with radically differing political philosophies.

*Sexism is a rising problem in my country, I would say. Korea is one of those lands where women were very much protected within the home and where the woman was looked down upon when she went out of the house to work. I would say that women have been and still are very oppressed, and if nothing happens to change that traditional oppression, it will go on the same way. In every place we have our own problems, and no one can solve another's problems for that person. We all have this existential pain in us as groups or as individuals, and I think it's the Christian's task to unite with others and tackle these problems out of love for one another.*

Liebje Hoekendijk, producer of a television program in the Netherlands, had as a young woman preached and led Pentecostal-type meetings in her country. She was invited to West Berlin as a press representative and all of her journalistic curiosity focused on the theme of the consultation.

*What would I like to see as I deal with the women in my society? I would like to have the whole role thing open. I mean everything that says, "This is feminine," I would say, "What do you mean?" or "This is masculine," again to say, "What do you mean?"*

*You can have a conception of it for yourself, but there is no generally accepted concept of masculinity or femininity, so nobody should use those terms except in an*

16

*individual way. It's being a person that matters and not being "masculine" or "feminine."*

*What I mean is this, that as a professional woman I have very great trouble with most men that I work with because most of them can't stand women who are leaders. They become afraid of them. For instance, we have two men on our staff. I'm the director and our typing "girl" is a man, and that makes it very difficult for the other men to turn everything around. I feel very sorry for them that they cannot be free of their self-imposed role stereotype. A gathering like this should help us all.*

Anaseini Quionibaravi was rarely without a flower in her hair to complement the bright Polynesian shifts she brought to West Berlin.

*As a woman senator in the Fiji Islands, I feel that I am one of few women in my country who have found themselves in unique positions in a man's world. I used to feel very lonely and out of place when I found myself on committees that were dominated by men and structured the way men think. Even though I had finished university in New Zealand, I often had to act according to the way I FELT about many subjects, but this eventually brought the men I worked with to realize that what a woman can contribute is very valid, even though her knowledge of the subject in an academic way may be limited. Now I find that in committees, if I don't say anything, the men very often ask, "What do you think about this?"*

Jan Cormack had already been on the way several days covering more miles on her journey from Christchurch, New Zealand, than possibly any other participant in the consultation. Jan was quite sure that nothing she saw on her long journey could surpass the diversity and beauty of her islands.

*I think I have always been unconsciously aware of sexism, although I didn't know that word until just recently. I have always been strongly aware that I would, and should, do what I wanted to do, and this probably influenced my decision to go into the church. I served as a director of Christian education and traveled extensively for the Presbyterian church to work with Sunday school teachers and leaders in the congregational education programs. I soon learned that people thought that deaconesses and church workers like me "took to the church" when they hadn't "found a man to marry"!*

*But I was never worried about that, and when I married I was fortunate to have a husband who recognized that I could never be just at home dusting the furniture and insisted that I go on with my abilities in education and music. It's tough for women who don't have understanding husbands or enough money to get away once in a while to develop other areas of their lives if they need that outlet, and most active and intelligent women find being confined at home constantly rather unbearable.*

Frieda, a young German pastor, hoped to be able to come to the consultation but was afraid that her parish duties would allow her to stay there for only part of the time.

*It takes a long time for church people to see the pastor as a woman in the fullest sense even though they are kind and pleasant. So many years of thinking have produced this attitude. The married women especially—and more especially the German housewife who makes a profession out of cleaning, cooking, and children—appear to be uncomfortable with the single woman and don't quite seem to know how to relate to her. I think it would make*

*them all feel better if I married, even though I am per-*
*fectly happy as I am. I don't think they quite believe that.*
*Part of the discussion of women's role must deal with*
*the acceptance of single women as "whole" people.*

Off the left side of the plane the aurora borealis danced across the polar sky just before dawn edged the eastern horizon with a thin line of light. A flight attendant, busy taking breakfast orders, found herself totally unable to communicate with the woman in the seat ahead of us, whose gray hair was covered with a black kerchief.

The Peace Corps worker to my left recognized her language as Persian and offered to act as interpreter, to the delight of all listening. The elderly Iranian wanted to make sure that as a Moslem she did not have any pork on her tray and was much relieved at being able to make this need understood.

I fell asleep to the rhythm of the M.P.'s snores on one side and the babble of Persian on the other. Frankfurt was four hours away.

*2*

# Her Awakening

The long ride from the Tempelhof Airport in West Berlin to the suburb of Spandau was a good opportunity to see some of the reconstruction that has taken place since those frightful years when there was no shalom in that war-torn land. The journey was a meaningful prelude to a consultation where women were gathering to assess the possibilities of reconstructing personal and corporate goals in the context of new understandings of the gospel.

The sixty buildings of Johannesstift had been miraculously spared during the bombing of Berlin. Founded by Johann Hinrich Wichern in 1858, the community took permanent residence in Spandau in 1910 and now employed 870 workers to staff its three hospitals, care for its 500 old people and 350 children, and to carry on youth-hostel activities. Its dedication is to the Word of God through a social-work ministry for the Evangelical Church in Germany.

The Christophorus-haus where we were to stay was a large three-storey building with two wings joined by the dining and lounge areas. I shared a room on the third floor which looked over a very pleasant garden area outside the dining room.

About a block away was the auditorium where general sessions were held. The assembly hall was set up with tables for delegates and the press with translation equipment at each place. A large crucifix on the brown curtain behind the speaker's platform centered the attention of participants. A profusion of living plants and flowers were the only other addition to the decor.

On the paneled walls printed messages in poster form proclaimed their interpretations of the theme of the consultation:

### SOROMUNDI
#### (Sisters of the World)

Woman's Place is in the House
   . . . and in the Senate

   I swear it to you
   I swear on my common woman's head
   The common woman is as common
   As a common load of bread. . . .
   *and will rise.*

   Turning through time
   workwoven
   the history of women
   is a world
   to be fought for.

The women who gathered in that room for the opening worship service created a living tapestry which vividly illustrated one banner whose cheerful prophecy was that *Sisterhood is blooming, springtime will never be the same!* Every hue and tint of the human complexion blended in a delegate body clothed in every imaginable variety of dress, from functional blue jeans and T-shirts to the delicately embroidered *kabaya* and sarong of the Malay countries, from British tweeds to wraparound skirts of African cotton.

These garments clothed women from most of the major church denominations and every political persuasion, among them lawyers, judges, university professors, social workers, pastors, missionaries, social researchers, church executives, theologians, housewives, psychologists, senators.

No men were invited to the consultation. Except for those technicians who helped operate the equipment and some newsmen and photographers, there were no men at the working sessions. In an opening night keynote speech, Dr. Philip Potter, General Secretary of the World Council of Churches, addressed himself to this situation.

> It may well be asked why this consultation is for women only. I am ashamed to say that this was absolutely necessary at this stage in history. While the World Council has always emphasized the co-operation of men and women in church and society, and the committee responsible for this concern in the WCC was made up of men and women, there is no doubt that women have not had the chance to speak clearly, fully and radically to the whole Christian community.
>
> It is part of the very nature of "sexism" that we men have dominated the discussion about women. We who have been the oppressors have pontificated on the role of women sometimes perversely, often

patronizingly. We are incapable of understanding from within what sexism means because we are mainly responsible for it.

And women have for too long acquiesced in our masculine judgements and attitudes and helped to perpetuate them. We have discovered in the struggle against racism that only the racially oppressed can really liberate themselves, and in the process they will help towards the liberation of the oppressors. This is what women are realizing over the world today. They must, under God, take their destiny in their own hands. This consultation is a significant ecumenical contribution to this process.

The liberation of women will mean the liberation of men. Booker T. Washington, the Black American leader, referring to racist oppression, once said: "You can't keep a person in the gutter without remaining there." The same can be said of sexism. Neither men nor women will become truly human unless this disease of sexism is diagnosed and cured. It will be one world of men and women or no world at all.

Sexism, like racism, is sin. Only in Christ can we become renewed to be authentic human beings, as men and women. But our life in Christ needs to be made real and manifest in our life together in church and society. As Dietrich Bonhoeffer wrote here in Berlin just before he was executed: "We shall only *know* what we *do*." It is my earnest hope that this consultation will be an ecumenical act which will enable us to know and do what is right in achieving a fuller humanity as women and men.

Dr. Potter's perceptive and hopeful words must travel a long way before they are implemented if the words of

Judy Sidden, a secretary at WCC headquarters in Geneva, are an indication of the pervasive sexism which currently exists there. In a paper circulated with the title *Sexism in the World Council of Churches or View From a Grade-Two Desk,* before the June consultation, she writes: "Not to my surprise, but certainly to my dismay, however, I found that the awareness and concern for the women's movement is very, very low, relative to the general awareness expressed in so many other arenas. Indeed, as one of my colleagues said to me shortly after my arrival, one of the first problems of consciousness-raising in the WCC will be to try to persuade people simply not to laugh or smile their condescending smiles when the subject of women's liberation is brought up."

The words of Dr. Potter and perceptions of Ms. Sidden indicate why the majority of women present agreed that at this point in time they needed to come together by themselves to chart their own course toward wholeness. We are still too close to our own awakening to permit anyone else to assist in our new definitions.

One of the most hopeful indications of awakening self-awareness was the ease with which each woman at the consultation was able to introduce herself as an individual apart from other relationships. Church women—in fact, women in general in the U.S.—have a way of introducing themselves primarily as "the daughter of," "the wife of," or "the mother of." It seems to be quite difficult to simply say one's own name.

Women are learning to say their own names as the simple statement of who they are. We are reminded of God's reply to Moses when he asked, "Who shall I say sent me?" And God said, "Say that *I am* has sent me to you." Whereas women historically have obtained their primary identity from their relationship with a father or a husband or some powerful man with whom they were linked, many are now pleased with their own individual completeness.

We are learning to appropriate the words of Christ to many of the women whose lives he touched, "Your faith has saved you (or made you whole); go in peace (shalom)." Johs. Pedersen says that this basic sense of *wholeness* or *completeness* is the fundamental meaning of shalom as "totality; it means the untrammeled, free growth of the soul," and designates "at the same time the entirety, the fact of being whole, and he [she] who is whole." [2]

Woman in her new shalom self is moving out of the historical context in which she was thought of as half a person unless she were married (a fact which has also been true in a lesser sense of unmarried men). Marriage must be proclaimed as the union of two "whole" individuals coming together to form a new "whole" rather than as two incomplete half-persons becoming "one."

### The Birth of the Shalom Woman

Theological liberation for women is a new birth into wholeness. Appropriating the wholeness of the image of God in which she was created (Gen. 1:27) and the fullness of new birth into the likeness of Jesus Christ (John 3:6), she experiences the revelation of her own "new creation" (2 Cor. 5:17).

From that point on she moves with autonomy, choosing her own way, making her own decisions, asking her own questions, sorting through her own answers. Being able to stand alone with "I am" as one's only identity places one in a position of great jeopardy, and many women retreat from this position, preferring the more comfortable although restricting existence defined by another person's identity. Traditional roles and submissive postures are seen as less threatening to one who has not yet stepped into the wholeness of shalom.

Wholeness embraces a certain solitariness. Carl Jung's description of this state, although masculine in gender, applies also to women at this point. "The man whom we can with justice call 'modern' is solitary. He is so of necessity and at all times for every step toward a fuller consciousness of the present removes him further from his original *'participation mystique'* with the mass of men—from submersion in a common unconsciousness. Every step forward means an act of tearing himself loose from that all-embracing, pristine unconsciousness which claims the bulk of mankind almost entirely." [3]

For many women this tearing loose from the unconscious bulk of humankind has been an "aha" experience. It's a moment of seeing the truth about oneself, of becoming fully aware. Like the moment of being born into Christ, it is an existential encounter with one's own wholeness. Having experienced such a moment, the newly-born shalom woman can never be the same again. Exploding with her new self, she is unable to return to the old dimensions of existence.

In a year when separate vocations and his illness forced my husband and me to live 2000 miles apart, I found that integrity which came as a result of having to rely solely on my own resources and the strengthening Spirit of God. I came to a new sense of self-respect for my own wholeness as a human being, my own ability to cope with myself and the needs of my situation. I covet now this same sense of autonomy for other women.

Anne Morrow Lindbergh documented in the book *Gift from the Sea* her lonely vigil on the beach when she claimed again her own being and her oneness with God and the natural environment.

26

Frequently there is this real need to get away from everyone in order to explore who one really is. But the fear of not being able to "make it on my own" haunts many women. As they move from one protected environment to another—from father's house to husband's house to children's homes in old age—a secret anxiety gnaws at their security: *what if there is no protected environment to which I can go if the one in which I now exist fails?*

The banner which says, *You can fly, but that cocoon has got to go,* challenges every woman to identify and break free of whatever it is that keeps her from knowing who she is in the sight of God.

To become a self-sufficient adult remains the goal of every life; to be one's own free agent relating out of strength and independence to every other human being is the challenge of maturity.

But here the shalom woman comes to the edge of the abyss.

Now she must part with the historical mold into which her life has traditionally been cast. She becomes that "unhistorical" person described by Jung as estranging herself "from the mass of men who live entirely within the bounds of tradition. Indeed, he is completely modern only when he has come to the very edge of the world, leaving behind him all that has been discarded and outgrown, and acknowledging that he stands before a void out of which all things may grow." [4]

Facing this frightening void, the shalom woman longs to share her experience but she is no longer comfortable or compatible with the traditional woman, unconscious and unaware of who she really is. She steps out into the void, dependent on God's Spirit to comfort her and on the support of other women in the same situation. The traditional woman simply cannot deal with the new questions these women are asking and retreats into safe cliché situations and into the repetition of ancient definitions.

The shalom woman discovers very quickly the applicability to her new situation of the words of Jesus that "new wine cannot be contained in old wineskins"!

In the process of discarding the old wineskins of tradition, she must pay the price of a sense of sin and guilt just as Jesus was pronounced a sinner and condemned to die for his proclamation of a new order of existence. The shalom woman must be prepared to walk the same path.

Again, Jung's modern "man" speaks to her: "An honest profession of modernity means voluntarily declaring bankruptcy, taking the vows of poverty and chastity in a new sense, and—what is still more painful—renouncing the halo which history bestows as a mark of its sanction. To be 'unhistorical' is the Promethean sin, and in this sense modern man [woman] lives in sin. A higher level of consciousness is like a burden of guilt." [5]

The shalom woman must be prepared for a period of trial and rejection, as the inevitable reactions come from both women and men to her revolutionary assertion that woman can stand alone, as a whole person, secure in her own definition of her role as woman.

## *Shalom Overcomes the Historic Soul/Body Split*

Students of the classics are familiar with the philosophical premise that all of nature represents a duality which might be summed up as the soul/body split. Ultimately, through the writings of men like Plato, the female nature was identified with body or matter, and the male nature with soul and rational ego. Body/soul dualism and female/male dualism became interchangeable concepts.

The soul (male) was conceived of as imprisoned in the body (female). Salvation lay in the soul's being freed from the brutalizing and corrupting influences of the body.

Dr. Magdalene Hartlich, M.D., a practising psychotherapist in Tübingen, West Germany, a specialist in group therapy and family counseling with much experience in youth care and preventative health care for mothers and children, addressed herself to this historical misunderstanding of human nature.

> For centuries we women have been kept in the isolation of the home; we have been taught to regard ourselves as beings with a lighter brain and less intelligence, with inferior independent creative ability and lacking an active independent will. Above all, we allow ourselves to be regarded, at once despised and glorified, as the embodiment of earthy passion and lust which drag the spirit and soul in the dust to their destruction.
>
> The emotional terms in which philosophers and theologians couched this image gives us some idea of the forces the males of our culture had to call upon to achieve the separation of spirit and body, heaven and earth, time and eternity. In order to keep their own human corporality, the richness of their human feelings, and their own sensuality suppressed by their fragmentary male existence, they had to declare that these vital forces belonged to the opposite sex. They had to project on to women characteristics, needs, and attitudes which are in fact natural to both sexes, simultaneously despising and cultivating them in her.
>
> And for a long time we "child women" thought

29

that the unequal treatment meted out to us in education, profession and politics was intended as fatherly protection against the realities of harsh and hostile life!

Classical dualism would not have had such a profound effect on the life of women in the church if the early church fathers and later on the Catholic theologian Thomas Aquinas had not absorbed it into Christian theology. Following Aristotle and Plato, Aquinas wrote that the female is defective in her nature, a "misbegotten male." [6] According to him, the father supplies the "formative power that is in his semen" to the child, while the mother provides only the soil or matter in which the seed is planted.

As Frau Dr. Hartlich pointed out, this was understandable in a day of inaccurate scientific knowledge. "This appears to be the moment in history, when the male finally came to feel himself entirely superior to the female and to assert his rights over her; his seed was visible, no one even remotely guessed at the fertile ovum of the woman. Thus the man received the wrong impression and with it the enduring claim that he was procreating himself in the woman, that he sowed his seed in her to grow and ripen."

The shalom woman refuses to accept either classical or theological dualism as the answer to her nature but reclaims her divine heritage as complete mind/body/spirit at the hands of God!

She clings tenaciously to the rock of God's grace in Christ, "For freedom Christ has set us free; stand fast therefore, and do not submit again to a yoke of slavery" (Gal. 5:1).

In a very real sense the shalom woman insists on "getting it all together."

## Walking as a Shalom Person

Whether female or male, all need to fight the demonic urge to be little gods. Was this not the essential ingredient of original sin as it's exposed in Genesis 3? "You will be like God," the serpent tempted (v. 5).

In her struggle to walk as a whole person, woman must resist the urge to claim and assert superiority and authority over men just as men must resist the temptation to exalt themselves as gods. Philippians 2:5-7 pleads with each one to have the mind of Christ who emptied himself of equality with God to become a "servant." Men and women must become each other's conscience lest we be tempted to sin in this respect. "Be subject to one another out of reverence for Christ," the apostle urges in Ephesians 5:21.

The shalom woman will reject the win/lose mentality and competitive spirit which taints male-dominated institutions. For her, *being* and *relating* must transcend *conquering* and *subduing*.

The secret of Christian freedom, said Martin Luther, is to be servant to all but slave to none.

As she learns to walk autonomously, there will be tugs to go back to the old doormat existence, and there will be tugs toward domination of other humans. In the uncharted "no-man's-land" of her new wholeness she must chart her course through experimentation with new situations and in the midst of the ever-present risk of failure.

Until she can walk free of both domination and submission, the shalom woman will be unable to contribute her complete potential to personal and societal relationships.

The shalom woman is any woman who will not settle for being less than God has called her to be.

*3*

# Her Theology

Seeing the Berlin Wall for the first time was a much more heartbreaking experience than I could ever have imagined it would be. That impassable barrier stands as a poignant symbol of all the barriers which have divided humankind. Presided over by armed guards and with a rotating pipe at the top to reject the desperate clutches of escaping hands, it slithers snakelike through the heart of the city and injects the poison of fear and distrust into its inhabitants.

Responding to pressure from Geneva, the German Democratic Republic (GDR) permitted two women to cross the barrier and to participate in the consultation. One of them was to deliver a major address; the other was to participate in group discussions. Their presence witnessed to the hope that in Jesus Christ all barriers can some day be broken through and all partitions transcended.

The question before the people of God as they face

the Berlin walls of human existence was articulated clearly at the consultation: Can the church embrace a theology of wholeness which reflects and is productive of oneness in Christ? Can Paul's brave declaration in Galatians 3:28 that we are all one in Christ—Jew/Greek, slave/free, male/female—become a reality for the church even though its edges are frayed and its truth tarnished by history?

On Tuesday morning of the week-long meeting, Nelle Morton, Associate Professor of Christian Education Emeritus of Drew University's Theological School in the United States, spoke on the subject, "Toward a Whole Theology." Professor Morton has lectured in several theological schools in the U.S. and has written numerous articles and made contributions to several books on the women's movement. With her white hair tied at the back of her head with a bright colored ribbon, Nelle Morton's entire bearing said, "I am proud both of being female and of being old!" as she articulated clearly some of the issues basic to a discussion of wholeness in theology.

> *Whole theology* cannot come through the western world alone, nor the eastern, nor from any control group speaking out of their experience as if it were the experience of all the people. *Whole theology*—as full human experience—is only possible when all the oppressed peoples of the world can speak freely out of their own experiences, be heard and touch one another to heal and be healed. . . .
>
> We come in our own right, as women, to claim our share of an inheritance promised long ago. And this pentecostal power of our presence calls into question any system, whether in church or in society, that tends to control and manipulate that

inheritance and our human destinies rather than to liberate them. . . .

We experience a common non-history. The world's understanding of itself and record of its development has not included women. Nor have church historians included us. A history that is not objective and does not embrace all its people must be seen as a partial history. Our partial history has provided us with male models only. Without historical memory one has no future and a limited present. But everywhere we are beginning to get in touch with our stories and to recreate our lost history. They form a new kind of history—not of great men, or great events, or even great women, but a history of the most common masses of people. . . .

Perhaps the greatest pain women bear from the church is being pushed to the periphery of the church's life and ministry. This brand of sexism is enemy to both men and women. It has robbed the church of its vitality. It has rendered the male-control group deaf to what is basically amiss in society. Sexism is one message of the church the world has not failed to hear. . . .

How timidly women have said, "I am minister!" How apologetically, "I am theologian!" Yet by virtue of Baptism every one of us is minister. And by virtue of being minister, compelled into the theological task. We may not be technical, systematic, or academic theologians. But we are in ministry and in the theological process and have much to do and to say and a new way of doing and saying. It will prove dangerous to the structures of the church for it will open ministry to the entire laity.

And should that happen, something, somewhere, would have to give. . . .

Since we are in process one can only speculate on the shape of a whole theology. But of one thing we may be sure. It cannot come out of one group or one sex speaking for the whole. Women cannot speak for the whole any more than men have not been able to speak for the whole. A whole theology would envision all of the people speaking out of their own experiences into the process and toward full humanness. . . .

Long ago the Judeo-Christian tradition envisioned a new history, inclusive of all people, and at home with the natural universe: peace to replace warring, justice and love to govern human relationships, and a new heaven and a new earth to replace the present competitive, exploitative one, when God's image (male and female) in humanity would be actual and apparent.

Were the entire human community taken with dead seriousness in our theologizing, there might be no more temple—for God would be in the midst of the people. The personal could be recognized for the political it is and the political, personal. A new heaven and a new earth would indeed appear—for the old heaven and the old earth *are already* in process of disappearing.

Whole theology is not a new fabrication. It deals with what has been there all the time. The imagery which needs to be kept in mind as one talks about moving toward a whole theology is that of someone regaining a lost inheritance or reclaiming a stolen birthright. It's a progress report of someone recovering that which has been spirited away by stealth or corroded by neglect.

The woman once again sweeps her house, this time in search of her lost theological identity, and as she sweeps away the cobwebs of theological neglect, it shines out as brightly as a new coin in all of the great events on which the faith is based!

## Women and the Image of God

The Scriptures tell us that female and male came into being *out of the nature of God* and as a result of the spoken creative word. Genesis 1:27 clearly asserts this fact. Now then, if God created the female as well as the male in God's image, then God must have a female as well as a masculine image.

Is that not part of the woman's lost inheritance?

Can we scrape away some of the corrosion of centuries of theological neglect and expose once again the whole nature of God?

The theological damage that has been done to the Body of Christ may be so severe that the church may never be able to deal rationally with the subject of the whole nature of God. So conditioned are we to hearing God referred to as male that we have problems even with Christ's assertion to the woman of Samaria that God is a Spirit (John 4:24), since a spirit in no way implies a corporeal male body.

But did not Jesus call God "father"? Was he saying that God is a father in masculine form or simply in a new relationship? Or were the medieval theologians correct in their discussions of the anatomy of God when they depicted a human body with male sex organs? Is God a sexual being, either male or female? Of course not.

The inevitable anthropomorphizing of God must be reckoned with as a reality, however, rising out of our need to find our being in the being of God in whose image we are created. For that reason women are uncovering the feminine imagery of God where it inevitably surfaces in the biblical account.

Let's take a look at all of the "wisdom literature" in the Scriptures and especially the Proverbs. "Wisdom" as portrayed in these writings refers of course to the wisdom of God, "a divine attribute but spoken of as having an independent existence. Now the word for wisdom in Hebrew *(hôkmah)* is feminine gender, and this partly explains the remarkable fact that divine wisdom as personified in these writings is a woman. . . . making it clear that our authors were not embarrassed by the grammatical necessity of referring to divine wisdom as female." [7]

Bringing some intriguing new insights from his understanding of the Hebrew language, Richard Wurmbrand, a Hebrew Christian pastor, writes that when the angel appeared in a dream to Joseph, it instructed him to call the child born of Mary, Jesus, which is in Hebrew the name "Jeshua," again a feminine word. "It is as though we were to call a boy Helen or Katherine. A man with a female name. It was this mystery which was expressed in the outward appearance of an Orthodox priest: he had to have a beard, but wear a woman's robe." [8]

Out of his experiences of 14 years in a Communist prison cell in Rumania, Wurmbrand says, "Whenever I feel God near me in this solitary cell, I always have the impression that there is also a female presence. St. John the Evangelist, in conditions similar to mine, alone, exiled on Patmos, saw God sitting on the throne. . . . But there also appeared to him in heaven what was to him a great wonder, as it was to me: 'a woman clothed with the sun and the moon under her feet and upon her head a crown of twelve stars.' Commentators make all

37

kinds of guesses as to who this woman might be. We have the explanation in the very beginning of the Bible: 'God created man in his own image, in the image of God created he him; male and female created he them.' This is the image of God: male and female. So there is a female principle in Godhead. The Kabbala calls it 'the Matrona.' God has all the perfections; he cannot be limited to the male ones." [9]

Therefore, concludes the Catholic J. Edgar Bruns, "There is no more reason for Jews or Christians to think of God as masculine (I mean independently of the purely literary and cultural influences which determined the kind of terminology used in our Scriptures) than as feminine." [10]

## Women and the Incarnation

There would have been no "incarnation," no birth of a baby in Bethlehem, had it not been for the woman Mary. Mary, the only human involved in the conception of Jesus, was acting as her own free agent, the Scriptures tell us, fully aware and conscious of what she was agreeing to, even questioning the procedure to be used in the conception of her baby (Luke 1:34) when she chose to cooperate in God's redemptive plan. She did not ask her betrothed husband's permission, nor did she seek counsel from a priest or other temple authority.

Mary is no meek and mild girl-child, but a strong shalom woman, free to express her faith in God in spite of the social stigma involved in her premarital pregnancy. Her Spirit-inspired song, called the *Magnificat* from its first word in Latin, sings of this faith in a God of personal concern and social justice and has become a manifesto of Christian values which the entire church might well adopt as creed in a world still crying in pain from the same needs (See Luke 1:46-55).

This aspect of Mary's nature, hidden under her role as Virgin Mother, has not been given historic recognition but, in a surprising 7000-word document which ruffled centuries of tradition, Pope Paul VI wrote to all Roman Catholic bishops on March 22, 1974, the following message:

> The modern woman will note with pleasant surprise that Mary of Nazareth, while completely devoted to the will of God, was far from being a timidly submissive woman. . . . On the contrary, she was a woman who proclaimed that God vindicates the humble and the oppressed and removes the powerful people of this world from their privileged positions.

The French Jesuit who introduced the document to the press interpreted this as meaning that women would attend assemblies of churchmen in a new role in the future. "The woman is bound to exert a decision-making power," he said.[11]

Whether one of the criteria for selecting such women will be their willingness to second male decisions remains to be seen. If they resemble Mary, they will act independently as God leads.

### Women and the Ministry of Jesus

If, in the days of his earthly ministry, Jesus Christ had in any way reaffirmed the religious view of women which existed in his day, no shalom woman could ever have given herself wholeheartedly to becoming one of his followers. The fact that so many *did* follow him clearly evidences that Jesus came piping a glad tune of newness for women. (See Luke 8:1-3 where women follow-

39

ers are listed by name as accompanying him along with the twelve male disciples when he went "through cities and villages preaching and bringing the good news of the kingdom of God.")

Contrariwise, the fact that so many churchwomen today accept unquestioningly, and even support vigorously, their own subordinate role in church structures, indicates that many of them have never really studied the Old Testament for an understanding of the status of women in the world into which Christ was born or studied the New Testament to ascertain Jesus' own attitudes toward them.

Why not check your own understandings of the nature and calling of the Christian woman against the following insights into the Scriptures?

1. *Jesus placed positive value on women as whole persons.*

In the Jewish theocracy, the law placed an economic value upon persons. This evaluation demonstrated their worth in pre-Christian Jewish society. Leviticus 27:1-7 lists these value judgments:

> The Lord said to Moses, 'Say to the people of Israel, When a man makes a special vow of persons to the Lord at your valuation, then your valuation of a male from twenty years old up to sixty years old shall be fifty shekels of silver, according to the shekel of the sanctuary. If the person is a female, your valuation shall be thirty shekels. If the person is from five years old up to twenty years old, your valuation shall be for a male twenty shekels, and for a female ten shekels. If the person is from a month old up to five years old, your valuation shall be for a male five shekels of silver, and

> for a female . . . three. . . . And if the person is
> sixty years old and upward, then your valuation
> for a male shall be fifteen shekels, and for a female
> ten shekels.

In a patriarchal society the evaluation of women as
being worth less than men was reflected in their lack of
legal rights, their lack of educational opportunity, their
inability to inherit property, and their lack of personal
worth. They were not permitted to study the Torah and
forbidden to enter into discussions with men, especially
in public. Prayer meetings could take place only if ten
males were present.

The low value placed on women made sons desirable
and daughters undesirable. Wives were considered the
personal property of their husband (see the Tenth Com-
mandment, Exodus 20:17), and could be divorced at
his will (Deut. 24:1-4) without recourse to a court of
law.

The birth of daughters made women ritually unclean
longer than the birth of sons. In this way, women were
punished for producing female children.

> The Lord said to Moses, "Say to the people of
> Israel, 'If a woman conceives, and bears a male
> child, then she shall be unclean seven days; . . .
> Then she shall continue for thirty-three days in the
> blood of her purifying; . . . But if she bears a fe-
> male child, then she shall be unclean two weeks
> . . . and she shall continue in the blood of her
> purifying for sixty-six days' " (Lev. 12:1-5).

In this cultural context, the strong affirmation of
women made by Jesus is revolutionary!

His assertion that women have rights in marriage as
well as men even caused his disciples to grumble, "If

such is the case of a man with his wife, it is not expedient to marry" (Matt. 19:3-10).

His lengthy discussion with the woman at the well of Sychar—the longest recorded conversation Jesus had with anyone—left his disciples totally dumbfounded: "They marveled that he was talking with a woman" (John 4:27). The "marveling" resulted not from his talking to a woman with a poor moral reputation, but simply from the fact that he was talking to a female of any kind.

When Mary of Bethany sat at his feet in the intellectual position reserved for male rabbinical students and her sister scolded Jesus for not telling her to come and help with the housework, the Lord said that Mary had "chosen the good portion" (Luke 10:42). As though in prophetic rebuke to the future church where women would be relegated again to the kitchen role, Jesus adds that this good portion "shall not be taken away from her."

Jesus was in no way putting Martha down as a person with these words because later on at the death of her brother Lazarus, Jesus engages her in one of the most profound discussions about his own resurrection to be found anywhere in the Gospels. To her he gives the revelation of himself as "the resurrection and the life" (John 11:27), and Martha responds, "I believe that you are the Christ, the Son of God, he who is coming into the world," an insight unsurpassed even by Peter's great confession in Matthew 16:16.

He refused to pronounce judgment on the woman brought to him with the charge of being caught in the very act of adultery, charging instead that men were not without sin and had no right to cast a stone at her (John 8:1-11).

He considered a dead 12-year-old girl as deserving of

being given new life as the widow's son (Luke 8:54-55; 7:11-17); he rebuked his disciples in favor of the mothers with small children (Luke 18:15-17). His regard for widows is well documented.

⅄ Without a doubt Jesus upset all of the Levitical valuation of persons. In his judgment women were every bit as valuable as men.

### 2. *Jesus denied motherhood as being the ultimate source of blessedness for women.*

In one of the crowds that followed Jesus wherever he went a woman tried to make this assertion about the mother of Jesus by calling out loudly, "Blessed is the womb that bore you, and the breasts that you sucked!" (Luke 11:27). In his reply to her Jesus insisted that "blessed rather are those who hear the word of God and keep it!" (Luke 11:28).

Again, this is not a put down of motherhood but simply Jesus' way of saying that we must put first things first and motherhood and fatherhood are not guarantees of blessedness either here or in eternity. Parenthood is simply one aspect of many human responsibilities.

### 3. *Jesus rejected the physiological uncleanness imposed on women.*

According to Leviticus 15, both men and women are unclean from their natural discharges—men if they had an emission of semen and women because of their menstrual discharge. Women were under greater pressure from these ritual laws because their discharges came with monthly regularity. After reading the description of the effect of her unclean periods on her social life (Lev. 15:25-33), every woman alive can empathize fully with the desperation of the poor woman who had suffered a "flow of blood" for twelve years (Matt. 9:20 *ff.*;

Mark 5:25 *ff.*; Luke 8:43 *ff.*). Anyone she touched became unclean until sundown; her husband became unclean if he slept with her; she was a social outcaste. No wonder she had wasted a lot of money on many doctors!

Now was it any wonder that she risked priestly judgment to touch the hem of Jesus' garment? Jesus seems almost cruel when he makes her admit publicly that she had touched him. His action, however, informs everyone there that he denies any uncleanness to himself as a result of her touch. (In light of this obvious repudiation of the old blood taboos on the part of Jesus, one wonders why many of the liturgical churches have for so long carried services for the "churching" of women after childbirth.)

Later, in the experience of Peter and Cornelius, the entire code of clean and unclean judgments was revoked by God (Acts 10:15).

*4. Jesus affirmed the feminine aspects of God's nature.*

In his three parables of the grace of God (Luke 15:3-32), Jesus pictures God as a shepherd (15:3-7), as a woman (8-10), and as a father (11-32). While making much of the shepherd image and the father image, theologians have somehow managed to lose completely the image of God as a woman! These pictures of God might even be said to explicate the nature of the Trinity. Since we would readily agree that traditionally God is father and Jesus is the good shepherd, then does it not follow that the woman seeking the lost coin is the Holy Spirit?

*5. The Gospels carefully portray women as well as men in their lessons.*

Luke records that at the Presentation of the child Jesus in the temple (2:22 *ff.*) there was a man named

44

Simeon who prophesied concerning the ministry of the Christ and there was also a prophetess named Anna (v. 36) who "spoke of him to all who were looking for the redemption of Israel."

Two persons, a woman and a man, who are not Israelites are acclaimed by Jesus as having great faith: the Canaanite woman whose daughter he healed of a demon (Matt. 15:21-28) and the centurion whose servant was healed (Luke 7:1-10).

When Jesus speaks of the condemnation that will come to his generation he says that two witnesses shall rise to testify against it in the judgment; the men of Nineveh and the queen of the south (Matt. 12:41-42).

Women as well as men must be watching for the return of Jesus Christ (Matt. 24:40-41), "Then two men will be in the field; one is taken and one is left. Two women will be grinding at the mill; one is taken and one is left."

Both sexes are directly responsible to God for the state of their relationship to him. Check the number of times he says the words *"Your* faith has made you whole . . . " to both women and men.

Space does not permit an exhaustive study of Scriptural affirmation of both sexes. But the affirmation is there in vivid illustrations of the truth that "God shows no partiality" (Acts 10:34).

Suffice it to say that Jesus was an unusual person, exhibiting both the so-called "masculine" and "feminine" traits in his life and ministry. He wept openly; he had great physical strength and lived a rugged outdoor life; he endured great pain; he did not "fight back"; he whipped the money changers in the temple; he was tender toward little children; he apparently enjoyed the company of women and men equally.

## Women and the Resurrection

As though in denial of the historical theological assumption that Eve was secondary in the original creation, Jesus selects a woman, Mary Magdalene, to be the "first person" in the New Creation! Even though Peter and John were at the tomb just moments before, Jesus waited until they were gone and until Mary was alone in the resurrection garden (John 20) before making his first appearance as the Risen Lord.

Mary and the other women are, furthermore, the only persons to be favored with a vision of the angels at the open tomb. None of the male disciples are given this privilege. The women are the first to believe the resurrection miracle, the first to proclaim it, and the first to be commissioned to go with the message. And for Jesus to give women the commission to bear witness to men was a radical departure from the whole Hebrew tradition which repudiated the witness of women.


## Women and Pentecost

The great freeing message of the Incarnation, the Cross, and the Resurrection was tucked away in the fears of the disciples' hearts waiting for the coming of the promised Spirit to release it.

When the Pentecostal outpouring came, Peter, moved by the Spirit, quoted from Joel 2:28-29:

> And in the last days it shall be, God declares,
> that I will pour out my Spirit upon all flesh,
> and your sons *and your daughters* shall prophesy,
> and your young men shall see visions,
> and your old men shall dream dreams;
> yea, and on my menservants *and my maidservants*
>   in those days

> I will pour out my Spirit; and they shall prophesy.
> (Acts 2:17-18)

In the Pentecost event more than in any other biblical record the church possesses a paradigm of liberation and a model for including all human experience in theology.

With the pentecostal dynamic let loose, all relationships were equally affirmed and people came together as equals in Christ, free from stereotypes, free from historic limitations, free from pretense, free from hierarchical patterns of dominance and submission.

Pentecost speaks to all people in a way that even the Exodus event cannot speak. The focus of its message is not just one race, one tribe—the descendants of the one man Jacob-Israel—it is for *all flesh*. All of the "gaps" that have been identified as separating some human beings from other human beings—men from women, the wealthy from the poor, the old from the young—are suddenly bridged, and God really dwells in the midst of the people and not in the templed orders. The vertical ecclesiastical ladder is shaped by God's action into an all-inclusive sphere with the Spirit as both center and circumference.

Pentecost marked the beginning of a new day, a day so new in its understanding of human relationships that the church has never really moved beyond its dawning.

But the message of Pentecost still lives, and the message is always this: God is not an "authority figure" who is "up there" and "out there," but a God who is "here," available to every class, age, race, and to both sexes. God is *Emmanuel*, "God with us," and the gifts of God's Spirit are directly accessible to all.

Freedom and liberty in the Holy Spirit can never be controlled by one group or one class. Freedom and liberty belong to God and to the Holy Spirit working directly through the gospel to free people to be all that God wants them to be.

**47**

For the sake of the life of the church it's imperative to restore the fullness of pentecostal possibilities to every person in the Body. Both gifts and fruits must be the right of each one to use for the good of all the rest of us. Only then will the church become the effective power it was meant to be. Competition will no longer rule in its ranks, and the "common good" will be its objective.

Post-Pentecost theology must always be dynamic and in process. Jesus tied us in to the Spirit of truth who will guide us, he promised, into "all the truth" and who "will declare to you the things that are to come" (John 16:13). The core of theological "truth" did not come to full expression in Pauline theology, in patristic theology, in medieval theology, in reformation theology, in Vatican II, but has been there all the time in the words and deeds of Jesus Christ. The church has only muddied the message.

Today, women moved by the Spirit of truth are not shrinking from declaring the "whole counsel of God" and are uncovering the shalom theology of the One who is our shalom. Its text will be written as the scriptures are lived out in the experience of the whole people of God.

*4*

# Her Church

On Sunday morning several double-decker buses waited at the Christophorus-haus to transport us to certain of the churches in West Berlin. I boarded the one destined for the Methodist church, the Lutheran Church, and the Moravian Church. The largest group of women on that bus disembarked at the first stop, and by the time we arrived at the Moravian Church there were just a dozen of us who got off. I had been tempted to join those who left the bus at the Lutheran Church, since smiling youthful pastors—one of them a woman—came outside to welcome their guests.

At the Moravian churchyard gate we were met by guides who led us down a short garden walk to the sanctuary door. Inside, white wooden benches and unadorned white walls created a clinical atmosphere. Smiling elderly ushers directed us to the various aisles. Being at the rear of the group, I noticed off to my right one usher standing alone and gesturing urgently for some of us to come his way. In order not to slight him, a young women from France and I responded to his invitation.

When it was too late to retreat, Hilde and I found ourselves the only women sitting on what was obviously the men's side of the church, innocently breaking a centuries-old tradition! The stares of the women across the aisle in the meagerly filled sanctuary were curious but not hostile, and one of the men in the pew behind us gave us his hymnbook. I found myself entertaining the delightful thought that everyone might be secretly rejoicing that the tradition had been broken so that henceforth they could be free to sit together in families!

I was also profoundly grateful that no lightning struck us nor did any thunderbolts break the stillness of the Sabbath morning to signify any divine anger. Instead it was "business as usual" at that service, and perhaps all that needs to be done is for women to test some of the traditions that have alienated men and women.

The history of the church is one of traditions being made and of traditions being un-made. Wherever traditions have evolved which are contrary to the gospel, they must constantly be challenged as to their intent and value. From the discussion in the chapter on theology it's obvious that the entire ministry of Jesus and the Spirit constituted revolutionary challenges to tradition.

### The Traditional Biblical Record

Given the record of Jesus' ministry and the ongoing enlightenment of the Holy Spirit, it becomes extremely difficult to understand how the "walls of hostility" dividing the sexes came to be rebuilt in the church structures. Christ's incisive words to Mary of Bethany promising that her new role should "not be taken away from her" (Luke 10:42) have been reduced to an inaudible

50

whisper. The prophetic voice given to women at Pentecost (Acts 2:17-18) has been muzzled by enlarging St. Paul's local disciplinary instructions into timeless ecclesiastical norms.

In defense of Paul we recognize that this great leader faced many practical problems in establishing Christian congregations in Hebrew and/or pagan cultures, not least of them being the tradition denying women legal recognition or opportunities for independent living. Paul did what had to be done in his day, but that day has long passed and with it the cultural conditions restricting the life of women at that time.

Today's woman does not need to be economically dependent on her father, her husband, or her husband's family all of her lifetime. She has access to academic learning and is able to develop the skills necessary to earn her own living. The wise use of family planning measures enables her and her husband to limit the size of their family in keeping with their own situation and with world population trends. Better health care gives her many more years of life and opportunity. Laws of primogeniture no longer are pertinent in the U.S., so there is no need to produce many sons to inherit property.

It's unfortunate then that the statements concerning the role of women in Paul's day have been used to enforce a rigid role pattern for women even some 1900 years later.

The definitive biblical norms for women in the church must be shaped by the actions and words of Jesus and by those statements of Paul which indicate his understanding of the gospel rather than his cultural conditioning. Basic, for instance, would be Galatians 3:28 where Paul states so positively that in Jesus Christ

51

sex differences no longer make any difference—we are all "one" in Christ.

Another example of this occurs in 1 Corinthians 11 where Paul has been discussing the cultural situation of women in Corinth. In the middle of his argument his sense of the gospel forces him to insert the parenthetical statement in v. 11 that *in the Lord* woman is not independent of man *nor is man independent of woman.* Paul is saying very clearly here that the deeper principle of equality in Christ is in opposition to the traditional cultural stance. The second verse of that chapter reinforces the fact that Paul is talking about two different things: one is tradition, the other is gospel.

In Ephesians 5, before he ever enters into a discussion of traditional Hebrew marriage relationships and their effect on the early Christian church, he posits a much more basic principle of "mutual submission" for wife and husband "out of reverence for Christ" (5:21).

Everything else that is said by the apostle which seems contradictory to full freedom for women in the church must be taken in the context of what is right "in the Lord." The culturally determined statements which apply only to the women of that day have no more validity now than the injunction to slaves which is found in Ephesians 6:5-9. Paul could not foresee an economy which did not depend on slave labor for its existence any more than he could foresee a world in which women would not be wearing veils as a sign of their marriage contract.

(Scholarly reservations about the Pauline authorship of Ephesians and the Timothy letters certainly have a valid textual base. We have chosen not to deal with these questions, however, since any analysis of the passages with which we are here concerned reveals their contradiction of Paul's understanding of the gospel.)

Especially difficult to reconcile with Paul's understanding of free grace is the passage from 1 Tim. 2:11-15, "Let a woman learn in silence with all submissiveness. I permit no woman to teach or to have authority over men; she is to keep silent. For Adam was formed first, then Eve; and Adam was not deceived, but the woman was deceived and became a transgressor. Yet woman will be saved through bearing children, if she continues in faith and love and holiness, with modesty."

The weight attached to Eve's actions in the Fall (Gen. 3) seems unduly heavy in this passage when compared with Paul's statements in Romans 5, which place primary responsibility on Adam. "Therefore as sin came into the world through one man and death through sin" (v. 12); "then as one man's trespass led to condemnation for all men" (v. 18); "for as by one man's disobedience many were made sinners" (v. 19).

The Timothy passage becomes increasingly perplexing in meaning when its theology is compared with John 3:16 where we're told by Jesus that "*whoever* believes in him" has everything he died to give! Yet in the Timothy passage other requirements are said to be necessary for women—both "childbearing" and "modesty." If childbearing is a requisite for salvation for women, then the status of unmarried women is particularly precarious in the church—especially if they don't bear a child!

A ridiculous interpretation? Nevertheless, to interpret the first part of this passage with its requirement of subordination and silence literally and not to interpret the latter section with its requirement of childbearing and modesty with equal literalness requires an intolerable confusion of hermeneutical principles.

The only sensible conclusion takes full cognizance of the large capital letter "I" at the beginning of 1 Tim. 2:12 where Paul says, "*I* permit no woman to teach or to have authority over men: she is to keep silent." Obviously this is another one of those church rules which Paul rather arbitrarily imposed out of his own cultural Hebrew conditioning. As opposed to the heavy use of the first person pronoun here, let us refer once more to 1 Cor. 11:11 and its assertion that "in the Lord" it is not so. There are times, then, when Paul speaks out of his own traditional authority structures and times when he speaks "in the Lord."

Paul's inconsistency in this matter is also evidenced by the contradictions between 1 Cor. 11:5, where he allows that women will prophesy but with veiled heads, and 1 Cor. 14:34, where he tells them not to speak at all.

The greater harm from assigning any long-term validity to the Timothy passage derives not so much from the enforcement of the rule that women should keep silent in the church (since it might be better for the church if all of us—men and women alike—kept silent more) but in the fact that it has forever linked women in the Christian church with the fall into sin.

Some serious questions present themselves for examination at this point. Was it really the intent of God that women should be defined in terms of Genesis 3 only? Didn't Jesus completely save women, too, and did he not give his Holy Spirit to them? If Jesus won for women a completed redemption on the Cross, then why does the church still treat them as though they exist in the unredeemed state when it comes to permitting them to exercise all of the options given by the Lord to his redeemed and Spirit-empowered people?

Yet the church continues to treat women as though Christ redeemed them in some lesser degree than men from the implications of the "curse" of the Fall. With very rare exceptions most of the articles written by men, most of the issue and study papers published, eventually get around to defining women's role in the church in the terms of Genesis 3.

By diverting theological attention away from pride and the desire to become like God as the essential factor in original sin, to sexual intercourse as epitomized in the "seductive" nature of woman, the church has succeeded in legitimizing prideful domination on the part of men and irresponsible submission on the part of women.

The awakening of woman to her full humanity compels her to repudiate the theological stereotypes which have been assigned to her historically as being false doctrine. She can no longer tolerate the evil dark-haired Eve image—the fallen temptress forever leading pure men astray, as the church fathers portrayed her. She is not Tertullian's "devil's gateway" destroying man, the image of God.

Neither will she be stereotyped as the persecuted "witch" of the Middle Ages, tortured and killed by the thousands during the Inquisition.[12]

Wholeness also compels the shalom woman to reject the opposing stereotype fostered by the historic church. She is not the perpetual "virgin mother" either, denying her own sexuality to become merely a body in which the foetus grows and develops. Sexual expression is claimed as good for reasons other than procreation alone, not least of all being her own joy and satisfaction in the act of sexual intercourse.

The virgin-mother image of woman has led to the notion that holier callings in the church are reserved for single and widowed women only. In fact some European churches which ordain women force them to renounce their ordination if they marry, a requirement not similarly imposed upon male clerics.

The shalom woman is claiming an entirely new definition of her role in the church by rejecting the word "role" entirely. *She is the church, and no role other than that which belongs to every other individual in that body can be assigned to her alone.* Her model is a composite of the Mary of the Magnificat; of Mary of Bethany who sat as disciple at the feet of Jesus and who poured out the costly ointment of her devotion in reckless disregard of public disapproval; of Mary of Magdala, freed of the demons of anxiety, fear, dependence, submission, inferiority, voicelessness, and self-hatred, persisting in the Garden of the Resurrection and being rewarded with a vision of new life!

By finding positive models in the New Testament church, the shalom woman regains her lost biblical roots. Even the few women mentioned in the Acts of the Apostles and in the epistles are so outstanding as to suggest that there were many other female leaders in the church who are not mentioned.

We know, for instance, of Priscilla who with her husband instructed Apollos, correcting his theology, and who is thought by some theologians to have written the Epistle to the Hebrews. Acts 21:9 tells us that the four daughters of Philip the evangelist were prophets. Lydia, a businesswoman, is credited with opening a new continent to the gospel (Acts 16:11-15). (How intriguing that God used a woman to bring Paul to the "man of Macedonia" of his vision!) Dorcas is the only adult raised from the dead after Christ's ascension (Acts 9:36 *ff.*).

Most fascinating of all is Phoebe whom translators identify as a "deaconess" (Rom. 16:1). The Greek word *diakonos* is used 22 times by Paul and is translated "minister" 18 times, "deacon" three times, and only in Phoebe's case is it translated "deaconess." Paul applies the title of *diakonos* to himself and to Tychicus, Epaphras, Timothy, and Apollos, all full-fledged pastors, preachers, and evangelists. According to the title Phoebe may have had all of these offices." [13]

As the church leadership sought temporal power in the Roman Empire, a male hierarchy developed which suppressed women. The Apostle Paul's local rules were made into universal norms, the church fathers projected their own sex fantasies onto women as scapegoat, and the church was off and running on a full-scale suppression of women as whole persons!

The history of that suppression has been documented thoroughly by many historians and theologians. The interested reader has only to check the bibliography in the final pages of this volume for more detailed information than it suits our purpose to repeat here. The West Berlin consultation did not deal to any extent with the historical church, choosing rather to concentrate on the contemporary situation.

The story of the church at this point in time reads pretty much the same from every part of the world. The institutional church is on its way toward full partnership for women but has miles and miles to go before it reaches that destination.

While some participants felt strongly that equality for women in the church could only come when it was guaranteed by the political system, the woman from the German Democratic Republic (GDR) was not so positive about this in her speech, "The Role of Women in the German Democratic Republic." Frau Christa Lewek, Secretary for the Church and Society Department of the Federation of Protestant Churches in the German Democratic Republic, holds the title "Oberkirchenratin." She is a member of the Evangelical Lutheran Church in Saxony and has held a variety of positions in key church departments.

One might consider why we have, for example, a Democratic Association of Women but no Democratic Association of men; an illustrated magazine for women, *Für Dich,* but no corresponding magazine for men. . . .

Within our churches at parish level, at worship and in parish activities we find the familiar outward picture in which women predominate numerically by far. But the "higher" the level we care to examine, the more the proportion shifts in favour of men. There is a gradual progression which can be observed from the parish council via the district church council to the regional synod, etc., in which more and more women fall by the wayside. In the synod of our Federation of churches, which probably still presents a favourable picture in overall ecumenical terms, of the 60 synod members 8 are women, and in the church leaders' conference of 28 members 3 are women. In the board, the highest administrative unit of our Federation, 5 men discuss and decide on their own. The intention here is not to create the false impression that a shift in the percentages would solve the problem. A quantitative change is certainly not the last word of wisdom! It is not a question of obtaining higher percentages for the participation of women but of possibilities for men *and* women to have a genuine influence on the processes of forming opinions and making decisions within the church. In this connection it is worth pointing out that the practical contribution of women to the administrative bodies of our church is already having a good effect. Their voice has a qualitative weight; their numerical representation is making gradual progress. We therefore have some grounds for optimism about our situation.

In a special post-consultation issue of *Risk*, the magazine of the World Council of Churches, Marnie Mellblom reports some answers given to her question, "How do you feel your church and your society value you as a woman?" Excerpts from their responses follow:

*One has only to refer to Vatican II, which recognized the fundamental question. . . . At the Bishops' Synod held in 1971, the Synod was asked to appoint a commission . . . to discuss the situation of women . . . and . . . this demand for a commission was made in the framework of the discussion on justice in the world. The commission was created by Pope Paul VI a year ago, and I am a member.*

> — Mlle. Maria de Pilar Bellosillo of Spain, President General of the World Union of Catholic Women's Organizations

*It is not a question of accepting or not accepting a woman if* she *does not make a personal effort to reach the heights of acceptance she wishes for herself. . . . It is not enough to want to be up there. There are a lot of responsibilities that go along with it. I think to serve the cause of true liberation it is for us to liberate not only ourselves but the communities around us, to accept us, to see us for our true value so that we can recreate a new pattern of living which will be better for all.*

> — Mrs. Leila Shaheen da Cruz, editor and manager of a publishing house and a member of the World YWCA Executive Committee, from Lebanon, Greek Orthodox

*I don't go to church anymore. . . . So I don't know how the church sees women, but I can imagine it is the same—sexism and racism go together and I think both are bad. I have never seen a woman minister even in the Ethiopian Church. Most of the women prayed at their Thursday groups, but on Sunday there was no female voice to be heard.*

> — Miss Zanele Dlamini, a member of women's section of the African National Congress, an exile from her country, South Africa

*In New Zealand, we women in the churches are not as oppressed as we think we might be. Most of the churches have opened the ministry of the word and sacrament to women. . . . I think the difficulty with us as women lies within ourselves. We are not ready to take our place; we are somewhat diffident about speaking out. . . . We should train ourselves to take part in decision making. We should become informed. We sit back a little too much.*

> — Mrs. Joan Anderson, a convenor of the Ecumenical Affairs Committee of the Presbyterian Church of New Zealand, and also the only woman on the Joint Committee for Church Union

*I have to say that the Korean church is not an exception, that we are denied certain positions. . . . Also, women are quite satisfied with conditions in the church as they now are. It is not the* MALE *that keeps women from assuming important positions but women themselves who form a force to discriminate against each other. For example, they do not accept ordained women as they do clergymen. And there is a sizable number of clergywomen in the Methodist Church in Korea. For the time being none of these women are doing pastoral work in the church. Instead they are helping with the women's societies.*

> — Mrs. Helen Hee-Kyung Chung, girls' high school principal in Korea, a Methodist

*The Roman Catholic Church is rather distrustful of women, especially those who are not members of religious orders. . . . My book,* FEMME ET L'EGLISE, *which appeared in 1973, was very well received. But . . . in certain Catholic journals, it was never mentioned. Why? Because in it I criticize those aspects of my church which are unjust to women. And also because I criticize St. Thomas [Aquinas]! . . . It is impossible for a woman to hold any key position in my church.*

> — Miss Ljiljana Mathkovic, writer and journalist from Yugoslavia, a Roman Catholic

*Recently the Anglican synod of the diocese of Jamaica met in the West Indies and a resolution was passed— and I must say, not without several dissenting voices— that "suitable women of the church can now offer themselves and be ordained as ministers." . . . It has taken a long time for this to be sanctioned. . . . Also the canons must be altered to allow the ordaining of Anglican women at the provincial synod which has not yet been held. In addition, no woman has to date been considered as a moderator, president, or bishop in the Jamaica church.*

> — Mrs. Doreen Kirkcaldy, a home economist in the food industry in Jamaica, member of the United Church of Jamaica

*In the United Methodist Church it is now possible for women and minorities to have acceptance and to participate at the decision-making level. However, we have not yet made a provision for women to become bishops. . . . In the ecumenical movement we find that many of the churches of the WCC still do not accept women except in certain roles—token roles and the traditional service roles. Within the WCC there is a great pressure for more women to be on committees and to participate in the Central Committee. I would say that at every level where I work there is great consciousness of this problem and that some work is being done.*

> — Clarie Collins Harvey, President of Church Women United, USA; Chairperson of Unit III, WCC; business executive and member of the United Methodist Church in the U.S.

## Women in Seminaries and in the Ordained Ministry

In 1957 a pastor of the Lutheran Church–Missouri Synod fervently urged all Christian churches to support the 1955 resolution of the Presbyterian Church, that "there is no theological ground for denying ordination to women, simply because they are women." [14] He concluded his book *Woman in the Church,* with this impassioned paragraph:

> Moses once expressed the wish, "Would God that all the Lord's people were prophets and that the Lord would put His Spirit upon them" (Num. 11:29). May God speed the day when these words become true; when, as Joel foretells, our sons and daughters shall prophesy (Joel 2:28-29); when, as David pictures the New Testament time, the host

of women preachers will be great indeed (Ps. 68:11), and when, as Isaiah predicts, it shall be our privilege in Christian pulpits everywhere to hear a woman herald of Good Tidings lifting up her voice to tell the Lord's Zion, "Behold your God!" (Isa. 40:9).[15]

It was not until 1970 that two of the Lutheran bodies in the United States voted to ordain women, while the Missouri Synod has still not done so. The majority of the world's Protestants preceded the Lutherans in ordaining women, although European Lutheran Churches have done so since World War II.

From these facts it might appear that women have at long last "made it" in the nineteen-century-old Christian church, and no one will deny that the ordination of women is a giant step forward in the realization of the promised "oneness" of Galatians 3:28.

None of the major discussions at the consultation focused solely on the ordained woman, although several participated on panels and in group discussions.

Frau Lewek, in her speech, affirmed the fact that ordination of women has not been a problem in the regional Protestant churches of the GDR "for a number of years now . . . women are ordained to the church's ministry and work as members of the clergy." However, Frau Lewek emphasized that "nowhere do they occupy senior positions in the hierarchy. Positions of leadership are still relatively seldom given to women in parish councils, district church councils, and other organs of the church."

This experience parallels that of clergywomen in the U.S. A survey reported by Church Employed Women, an organization related to the United Presbyterian Church in the USA, discovered that, of 67 out of 144 clergywomen:

— all in congregational positions were at the median pastor's salary for the entire denomination or lower, all the way down to nothing

— less than half listed having housing and pension benefits (which are usual for male pastors)

— about half received car or travel allowances

— only one-third had continuing education as a benefit

— only one-sixth listed vacation

— none get maternity leave or unemployment compensation

— those who work as co-pastors with their husbands (3) either receive half salary and half pension for full-time work or no salary and no pension but an annual baby-sitting allowance.[16]

A recent sharing of experiences among women pastors in the area of one U.S. city provides a valid microcosm of the situation for ordained women elsewhere in this country. In the area of Seattle, Washington, there are a few more than a dozen ordained women ministers in the "mainline" Protestant denominations.

In her article in *The Seattle Times,* reporter Sally Gene Mahoney says that often the "dying churches are the only ones open to the female minister, who then must preside over the death. There is the obvious danger that the woman minister will be blamed for the demise, which was coming long before she appeared on the scene."

Less than half of the ordained women in Seattle are in neighborhood churches where they are able to carry out all of the pastoral functions such as liturgy, preaching, marrying and burying, counseling, and youth work.

Some of the women ministers choose to work outside of the institutional church, feeling that these times are "dangerous" for women, and that it will be easy for them "to be seduced" by the hierarchical ambitions of the institution.

"When women achieve the position [in the church], it is easy for them to sit back and let someone else do it. That would be bad for both men and women. If women are taken seriously, we can create a whole new structure . . . create a new kind of world," says the Rev. Christine Morton, who with 4½ years of pastoral work behind her, has embarked on a ministry called *Entity*, which cooperates with groups within the broad church.

Not all of the women ministers in the Seattle area are sure that they would go through it again. "Although none spoke of discouragement, one can sense that most have met with both joys and sorrows in their ministry," says the reporter.

The Rev. Nell Carlson points out that "for women, an extra amount of nerve, courage and determination are what it's going to take."

In another context, the sensitive perceptions of Susan Barrabee, writing as a seminary student, sum up the situation for women seminarians as she sees it.

> As for the seminary as a whole, I cannot really say that I'm very optimistic. Seminary women everywhere are coming to consciousness . . . but there are few places where it is clearer that it is a man's world than in a seminary, and I see very few signs that men in these institutions are at all ready to take the issue seriously. . . . The seminary's ability to deal with women and the "woman question" is rendered somewhat irrelevant by the simple fact that no amount of enabling her to become

65

a whole human being and no amount of equipping her for ministry is going to matter as long as the institution within which she is to work—the church —makes no significant place for her in its theology, function, and structure. In the meantime we may discover that the energy spent in looking around for access to a place in a sinking ship would have been better spent in building a new one.[17]

Perhaps one of the keys to changing this pessimistic outlook lies in whether or not women in the ordained ministry are supported in their vocation by other women in the church. Women in congregations influence the attitudes of congregational call committees. If they overtly indicate any negative attitudes toward having a woman as pastor, the call committee will reinforce male leadership because "even the women don't want a woman pastor."

While some studies indicate that women are generally more negative toward women pastors than men are, I question the reasons for the responses given. I have personally questioned many church women, individually and in groups, and found them generally very supportive of women who want to be pastors. Their negativism when expressed is usually based on their comprehension of the difficulties which women who are pastors encounter and they prefer that their own daughters find careers which will leave them less vulnerable to hurt and disappointment.

The Seattle women agreed that one key to success for the woman minister lies in the backing of committed male clergy, of which there are a growing number who are willing to do more than give verbal assent to their denominational policy statements affirming full status for women in the church.

## The Traditional Women's Auxiliaries

The women's societies of the major denominations have until the last couple of decades been the only area in the life of the church open to women in leadership. Many of these have become very powerful political identities. They control large budgets and often manipulate congregational life through the amounts of money they contribute to benevolence offerings and through gifts of furnishings and equipment.

Until recently, most of them did little to influence directly the decisions of the male church leadership, nor were they concerned with participation in the decision-making process. While the auxiliaries are supportive of the programs of the church body, they have had little to say about the initiation and administration of church-wide programs.

They did make a very large contribution to the life of the women of the church by providing leadership training, Bible studies, and opportunities for education and involvement in the program and mission of the church. Largely because of their diligence in these matters and the fact that women have more free time for reading and meeting than men do, laywomen are generally better informed church members than laymen. This has been documented in *A Study of Generations* which summarizes research into the attitudes and actions of Lutherans.

> On all dimensions reflecting beliefs, values, attitudes, and behavior that may be regarded as positive, Lutheran women consistently show slightly higher scores than do Lutheran men. . . . In the area of religious practices women are more active in personal practice of piety and personal witnessing. They also have slightly more biblical knowl-

edge. Men show a greater tendency actively to express their personal views on controversial issues to authorities in both church and society. As a whole, women make a stronger showing on measures both of belief and expression of faith. Yet men tend to communicate their concerns more actively than women which may mean that the church is hearing the most from the group less highly identified with its faith and life.[18]

Now that women have been trained and are prepared for the broader areas of church leadership, church women's societies face a dilemma which only they themselves can resolve. This dilemma can be stated most simply in these two questions:

1. Shall church women's societies do all they can to become increasingly autonomous, independent, and politically powerful, since it appears that it's going to be a long time before women have any representative strength as individuals in the church policy and decision-making areas?

2. Does the existence of church women's auxiliaries constitute a hindrance to the full participation of women in church-wide decision-making by providing a quasi-ecclesiastical parastructure?

If the biblical ideal for the body of Christ is for women and men to be one in full human liberation, then why segregate one section of the body into an organization where the other does not serve? Does this not militate against wholeness? Would it not be better to encourage participation of women in the full life of the church and permit the auxiliary to be open to both men and women as a service organization? Or would this mean the irrevocable loss of the only political identity women have in a church which has been reluctant to permit them partnership in all of the areas of ecclesiastical life?

Probably only time will decide whether or not traditional church women's organizations will remain a viable part of the church's life. For some women, the auxiliary will be the only way for them to participate in the life of the church at all; for others, it will become even more a stumbling block to wholeness.

The shalom woman, while well aware of the political advantages of powerful women's auxiliaries, reaches out eagerly for the day when church structures reflect and produce a shalom community in which no functions are assigned on the basis of sex alone.

### Steps Toward Wholeness in Church Structures

Where do we start to exorcise the sin of sexism from church structures? Do we look first at the exclusively masculine language which dominates sermons, hymns, and liturgies? The shalom woman who has learned to appreciate her femaleness as a reflection of the image of God experiences pain whenever she is made to feel like a non-person at worship celebrations. A sermon addressed to "brothers" or "brethren" only, a creed which confesses faith in God's actions for "us men and our salvation," hymns which sing only of sons, brothers, and fathers—these are sending many women in search of congregations where pastors are sensitive to the exclusiveness of masculine language forms.

Then again, the first place to start may be the parish education curriculum and audio-visual materials which reinforce cultural role stereotypes.

What about being concerned with voting rights for

women in those congregations which deny them this basic right?

And how do we go about correcting the shocking scarcity of women in ecclesiastical decision-making bodies?

The objective of the task must be to demonstrate in all of the structures and events of the church's life the fact that in the Kingdom of God there are no second-rate citizens. The church which prays "Thy Kingdom come on earth as it is in heaven" cannot afford to waste any more time in making this petition a reality.

*5*

# *Her Relationships*

Blue buttons. I had looked for them at both the Frankfurt and Tempelhof airports. Each one of us had received one of the bright blue circles with our registration materials. On them was printed the Greek word *oikoumene* which translates into English as the word "ecumenical."

One other blue button was visible at the Tempelhof. The wearer spoke English, to the great relief of both of us, and introduced herself as a Canadian social worker, a member of the Anglican Church in Manitoba. We proceeded through customs together and after exchanging our currency for German marks we found a taxi to take us to Spandau.

Those blue buttons signified a relationship and a contract. They sealed our agreement to enter fully into the life of that particular ecumenical community for one week. Wearing the button indicated a vested interest in the theme of the consultation and consent to its being a valid subject for concern.

A certain assumption of risk was also involved in its wearing. Inherent in the consultation assignment was some vulnerability to possible misrepresentations on the part of the press and from those groups antagonistic to the ecumenical Christian concerns.

To me, the buttons spoke of shalom as covenant (berith) a concept with which it has a special kinship in the Hebrew. The covenant-relationship is a perfect expression of shalom in its meaning of wholeness. Those who are united through friendship or covenant, became shalom—whole with—one another in the kind of intimate harmony that members of a family know through their common birth.

This union of souls which creates shalom is illustrated beautifully by the friendship which existed between David and Jonathan (1 Sam. 18:1-5). In their friendship, shalom is so strong that the claims even of family must give way before it. Love, friendship, a sense of unity are in the covenant-peace; "to 'speak peace' with one another and to 'speak love' are two manners of expressing the maintenance of the common covenant; it is practiced by those who 'know' each other, because knowing indicates a thorough, mutual feeling." [19]

Before the week in West Berlin was over, many of us would have established a shalom covenant with one another, a never-to-be-forgotten relationship based on commitment to mutual goals. This is a problem that confronts those who make shalom with others: can respect for one another's differences enable community shalom without violating individual rights? Shalom relationships are contractual unions which respect the individual but exist for the common good.

Those unions must be based on honesty. The shalom woman cannot relate to anyone in a less than honest way. If a stereotyped role is not an honest one for her or is not compatible with her own personality, abilities, skills, education, background, or theology, then she cannot expend valuable energy playing that part. Putting on a performance, maintaining a pretense for the sake of satisfying role requirements written by others, constitutes a cheap little drama that cheats all the players.

It would be just as dishonest, for instance, to require all women to go out and be productive in managerial jobs or in trades for which they are not temperamentally or physically suited as it is to expect all women to be happy or comfortable doing such things as housework or gardening when neither aptitude nor interest qualify them for these pursuits. Even being a mother or a father in today's society is not something that happens naturally. It requires the same interest, motivation, and development as any other skill.

The shalom woman is asking the church and society to make it possible for women to exercise their honest options in all relationships.

### Relationships with Men

The basic human relationship is usually contracted with a member of the opposite sex. Sexual differences create the primary challenge for a shalom relationship. No other difference approximates this difference. Color, I.Q., size, and shape—these are all secondary to the basic opposition of maleness and femaleness.

Woman and man represent the primary polarity. Since we tend to like and to value others to the degree that they are like us, shalom between man and woman requires constant renegotiating. We approach each other with some suspicion over the other's motives, sparring for advantage.

73

"Never trust a man" is the warning given by many a good mother to her daughter, and "I just don't understand women!" is the message communicated by fathers to their sons. "Why can't a woman be more like a man?" is the plaintive wail of the professor in *My Fair Lady*. Girls chant the taunting, "Reuben, Reuben, I've been thinking, What a grand world this would be, if the men were all transported, Far beyond the northern sea!" And boys respond with, "Rachel, Rachel. . . . "

The polarity of the sexes is reinforced from the moment of birth. With the answer to that first question, "Is it a girl or a boy?" an entire set of cultural and traditional expectations is set in motion for that child.

We know them so well. Girls must act helpless; boys must act strong. Boys must be independent; girls must learn to be dependent. Girls must grow up to be submissive; boys must grow up to dominate. Boys must grow up to make lots of money; girls must learn to work just as hard for less or no money. Girls will be full-time mothers; boys will be part-time fathers.

All the machinery of cultural conditioning operates to produce a culturally perfect product. School textbooks depict cultural role models, television commercials dramatize them, and comedians base their routines on them.

Unfortunately, some valid questions about the whole process are never seriously dealt with: is this conditioning compatible with God's calling for individuals and with the child's innate characteristics or is it something imposed on both sexes regardless of individual potential?

Because these questions are ignored, a tragic situation develops as many men break down under the pressures of having to be a "winner," of having to stay "at the top," of having to be "worth a lot," of having to be the responsible person at the top of an imposed "Divine

Order," or of simply having to act aggressively and decisively when that is not their nature. Similarly, depression haunts many women who have great intellectual ability, much physical strength, or the capacity to administer well, but who are forced instead to subjugate all of this God-given ability and talent to play the submissive role which society and the church approve.

What a waste for both the female and the male child! With options limited from birth many can only look forward to a life of frustration and the waste of their resources. For those unable to cope with this drain on their emotional energies, alcohol, drugs, and suicide too often become a way out of their role dilemma.

I received a letter containing the following comment from a young pastor: "We find our most satisfying and challenging ministry here is with women 25-45 who are particularly puzzled about their worth as people. You tried to tell me that would be happening years ago and I doubted. Don't give up the fight. That I've been sort of converted is proof enough that miracles still happen."

God gave only two basic assignments to the human beings he created: 1) to subdue (organize?) the earth, and 2) to be fruitful and replenish it (Gen. 1:28). In both of these tasks the female and the male were to cooperate. God left it up to the human beings themselves to determine how they would do the job. Therefore in some cultures it's perfectly normal for women to do the hard, physical work while men sit around and do a great deal of talking among themselves. Even the oft-quoted Proverbs 31:10-31 illustrates this pattern! In other societies both are forced to share in all productive work and in decision-making. In western societies married women usually stay home and play more of a consumer role while men earn the living for the family and do most of

75

the productive tasks for the society. The life of the career woman, married or single, usually focuses much of the discussion about the role of women. This is particularly true when her career earns a high salary, since such careers have traditionally been reserved for males.

At the consultation many informal discussions on the subject of role relationships made mealtimes and tea times buzz with conversation. One of the more formal ones occurred between Anna Jiagge, a Justice of the Court of Appeals in Ghana, West Africa; Eva Zabolai-Csekme, an ordained pastor from Hungary who is now an executive with the Lutheran World Federation in Geneva; and Sarah Bentley, a U.S. seminary student. All agreed that the cultural background of a people had to be the context for understanding their attitudes toward women. They also observed that there does seem to be a difference between women's situations in agricultural versus urbanized societies and that such differences must always be taken into account.

Anna Jiagge noted a situation in her own country of Ghana which reflects a common experience in many countries including the United States. She pointed out that even after education became available to girls in Ghana, many women continued to keep their daughters at home because they preferred to train them to be in charge of a household. Although this changed somewhat after Ghana became independent, the result was that women started their education later than men; thus there are few women in government service, the professions, and all those areas of life that require greater academic training.

ANNA JIAGGE: In Africa, 80% of the people live in rural areas and work in agriculture. The main issue is the fight for existence. Where starvation is not far in the

76

distance, your struggle is to make ends meet in order to live. And in that struggle men and women participate equally, and that puts a completely different conception on their relationship. A woman is expected to contribute to the maintenance of the home, so that financially she has to secure herself some sort of occupation that will help her earn money. The total financing of the family does not come from the man alone, and where the woman contributes that, she has a voice in how the children are educated.

We didn't pass through that Victorian era when the woman was supposed to be weak, and so on, and have to be protected by the man.

INTERVIEWER: And you think you will avoid it? You will jump over that stage?

JIAGGE: I hope so. We don't want it.

INTERVIEWER: But to avoid it, you have to be very aware of it?

JIAGGE: We are aware of it—seeing you. We know the results; we know your problems and understand them.

EVA ZABOLAI-CSEKME: I wanted to contradict something you said before about it being a "luxury" that women can—have to—stay home. This word has something of a connotation that it is something very positive, something good, that we are enjoying, when in fact it turned out to be something bad, very negative, that women can or have to stay at home, because our entire social system is built in a way that it would not be possible for our men to work ten and twelve hours a day and be away from the family so long and produce so much, if their women would not stay at home and care for the family.

At the same time, this has taken away the so-called

"role of the women" which existed 200 years ago. At that time it was meaningful, at least more meaningful than it is today, for the women to stay home, because she was bearing all those children—ten, twelve —out of which half of them died. Those children were necessary for agriculture, to have workers for the field, and besides that, the women died when they were 45—and that was their life!

SARAH BENTLEY: But the home was a much more important part of the economy. They were running a mini-society at home. Even in our Middle Ages, the woman stayed home and ran a manor while somebody went off and (unfortunately) ran the Crusades; she ran a small village. She supervised the lives, helped in the community, of a whole bunch of people.

JIAGGE: And in that set-up she was not recognized as someone of an inferior status; she had place.

(At this point, Eva Zabolai-Csekme strongly questioned the assumption that women were highly regarded in the Middle Ages. Eva was making the point that the situation was more complex and not so easily categorized as positive for women.)

INTERVIEWER: Aren't you afraid that if an African country passes through this industrial life stage, the woman will lose this economic role which she now has? That's the real danger to me, unless people take strong measures.

JIAGGE: It's a real danger when only men sit in the decision-making bodies, but the danger is minimized when women also sit in the decision-making bodies.

INTERVIEWER: Do you think this is enough? Should positive measures be taken to insure that women will not be pushed aside in this process of modernization?

JIAGGE: What we say at home today is that it is *not* enough to provide men and women with equal opportunities in education. There have to be special incentives to keep the girls in school long enough to qualify and train for the skills.

From my background, traditionally girls married early in order to have lots and lots of children, and the traditional attitude is not in favor of women staying in school after they have reached the age of puberty. There has to be definite efforts to fight that attitude; otherwise you inhibit girls from going further and developing their talents to the best of their capabilities.

BENTLEY: I think it must help too, as you said, that you just came out of a period of struggle in which women and men were together. You are not coming out of a long history of inferior status. You've come through a different period in the last 25-30 years. [Women in Africa] have models; they've seen women in Parliament, and they see women judges.

INTERVIEWER: I want to go back to what you said about it being a myth that when women were productive at home, they were not so degraded.

ZABOLAI-CSEKME: I would agree that at the point when women were doing home economics, it was not defined in the terribly narrow sense that we have it today. It included the production of all kinds of household goods—wool and spinning, making clothes, woodcarving—whatever was needed for the family. Today you go to the store and buy these goods, so this is not the role that the woman is playing anymore.

Besides that, she was constantly occupied with bearing children because our women in Europe used to be childbearing machines, and they died very early, so

79

when they died, they still had small children. Today, when people have two or three children, by the time women are 40 or 42, their children are out of the house and into college, but women have still another 30 years to go!

If you teach them that your only goal in life is to raise children and care for your family, those coming 30 years are going to be meaningless, and these women are completely frustrated because it's a completely changed situation in our 20th century. That's why it's impossible for us to go back to that situation, and we don't want to go back. But on the other hand, we have to realize that our entire structures of society were built up in a certain way, and we have to change the entire structures in order to create meaningful partnership between the sexes.

JIAGGE: In our society, too, in the recent past, you got the labor for work on your fields or for your fishing business from the number of children you have, and so it was an asset to have lots and lots and lots of children. Now today, children go to school. Therefore, they are no longer income-producing; they are income-consuming and the incentive to have lots of them diminishes.

We have at the moment a very large group of women in the rural areas for instance, who were brought up to be good mothers and to maintain vegetable farms for the use of the house and for the sale of extra vegetables and crops for money to be spent on dimensions of the house. But they have no real skills that will earn them the amount of money they require for the education of their children. Our problem now is how to help these women, because modern life is changing Ghana so rapidly, and unless you are able to earn enough, you very easily and very quickly fall to the subsistence level. The effort now is how to use this reservoir of unskilled women in our country. That is the problem we are facing at the moment.

Given the facts of our individual differences and particularly our uniqueness as females and males in the constantly shifting kaleidoscope of history, the reexamination of old cultural contracts and the writing of new ones becomes mandatory. When ancient contracts are part of long-standing cultural traditions, changing them is especially traumatic. In the popular play *Fiddler on the Roof* the negotiating of new marriage contracts by his daughters shattered the traditional securities of the Jewish father.

Making new contracts for shalom relationships frequently finds one of the parties seeing no need for change while the other cannot go on unless the terms change. A young seminary student commented on the number of women in the psychiatric ward of the hospital where he was taking a summer course in clinical pastoral education.

"Many of them," he said, "are just depressed from being home all day with their husbands gone most of the time. They feel cooped up and wish they could spend time with other adults, but when their husbands come home, they're tired and don't communicate."

When asked what kind of treatment was given them in the hospital, he answered, "They were usually given sedatives to help them rest and counseling to help them cope with their situations. When they left, usually after a couple of weeks, they were given prescriptions for tranquilizers."

Many women today are looking at the terms of the traditional marriage covenant and observing that the changing culture has made shalom under the old terms impossible.

A century ago a majority of Americans lived in rural areas or small towns. (Like Anna Jiagge's Ghana now?) Usually homes were shared by more persons than are now included in our small nuclear family units: grandparents, single uncles and aunts, cousins, young hired workers who had emigrated from Europe, and all contributed in some meaningful way to the life of the household. In fact survival often depended upon each person in the family being engaged in some productive activity—spinning, weaving, canning, pickling, educating the younger children. All of these were part of the activities of the household itself.

Women of the family made especially vital contributions to the community life, as Rev. Zabolai-Csekme noted. They were the nurses of the ill, they provided for the burial of the dead, they were the midwives who delivered babies, they were the pediatricians who instructed younger women in the care of their children. Besides all that they assisted with the work of the farm and the care of animals.

If the family owned a small business, as many did, all of the members took their turns working in some phase of it. But, as in Ghana now, there came a time when the boys were sent off to school to be educated for leadership roles while the girls were still necessary contributors to the survival aspects of family life.

Belatedly, and largely for economic reasons, universities opened their doors to women students and the term "coed" became part of our vocabulary. Today, even though more women are college-educated than ever, the educational lag has never been overcome. Women have lost out in professional and business life, and at the same time the importance of their work in the home

82

has diminished. Because of the industrial revolution, food and clothing are produced or processed elsewhere; childbirth and child care are in the hands of professional doctors (usually male); and the burial of the dead is in the hands of male morticians.

And the list grows. From full-time producer of life's necessary goods, the woman has become a full-time consumer, cajoled, exhorted, wheedled, and shamed into buying more and more! Millions of advertising dollars are spent to praise the women who stay at home simply because stay-at-home women go shopping more often! Career women and women interested in such "masculine" concerns as business and politics do not waste money in shopping orgies. The term "housewife" (one who is married to the house and the work it encompasses) has become an empty term.

A majority of women are looking for a change in the marriage relationship, according to a recent poll which conducted hour long interviews with 3000 women and 1000 men representing a cross section of society. The poll was undertaken by the Roper Organization, Inc., in the spring of 1974. The same number of women representing a similar cross section of society had been interviewed in 1972 and 1970 and the results of both surveys compared. Of the 3000 women polled in each instance, a 57% majority now favored efforts to improve the status of women compared with 48% and 40% in the previous polls.

The institution of marriage itself does not seem to be under attack, because of the women polled, 96% consider marriage the most satisfying and interesting way of life, but what is "changing dramatically is the kind of marriage women say they look forward to—just any marriage at all will not do."

In the vanguard of change are "young well-educated

women . . . half of the college educated women and 61% of all women under 30 favor a marriage of equal partnership, where husband and wife both work and share homemaking and child care responsibilities. Women aged 50 and over favor a traditional marriage, where the husband is the provider and the wife the homemaker and child rearer." [20]

The president of the polling organization said that "his research leads him to conclude that conceptions about female roles are changing much faster than ideas about masculinity, and that women are a little more ready for such changes than men."

"Man," he said, "would seem to be next in line for liberation."

But men must first see that they *need* liberating. Perhaps before it's too late, they will examine their shorter life span, their susceptibility to heart attacks, strokes, hypertension, and other stress diseases and decide that the price they pay to be Number One is not worth it. They will look with compassion on the daughters and sons who are deprived of their parental time during their childhood and wish they had been with them more. They will listen to their wives and finally *hear* what they are saying and return to being human rather than to "playing god."

It will take time. In the meantime, back in the church, an authoritarian backlash is attempting to reestablish outmoded patriarchal patterns under such labels as "Divine Order" and "chain of command," terms which do not originate in Scripture. Although contrary to all that the gospel and Pentecost have to teach us about liberty and freedom, these movements are gaining adherents among those who find gospel freedom hard to handle and who look to tightly structured relationships to solve their personal problems.

84

The church must recognize this reaction for what it is—a modern day version of the attempt to silence women who are led to speak out on behalf of honesty and authenticity in women/men relationships. The fears of both men and women must be dealt with by each other in the light of God's grace and forgiveness as they move into a new shalom covenant, maintained with each one's wholeness in mind and not at the expense of one or the other.

### Relationships with Children

The relationship of the shalom woman with children needs also to be examined in the light of her relationship with men. As mother, she looks for father to be truly father, a partner in the entire parenting process. Although "mom" has been excoriated and the finger of society pointed to her as responsible for all juvenile problems, the role of the father cannot be minimized in its influence upon children. Cruel, domineering, neglectful absentee fathers must share responsibility for actions as they affect their offspring. Most middle-class fathers will disclaim being any of the above; but if they are totally involved with a life away from home, they will surely have a negative influence in the life of their children.

The shalom woman knows that the liberation of men also from the restrictions of their assigned roles would give them more freedom to participate in the lives of their children, too. Dr. Magdalene Hartlich addressed herself to this need:

> In this reciprocal process we do not have to compete with the men and cultivate the so-called characteristics of the opposite sex. We should not adopt

the male role of strength and domination, freedom from anxiety and suffering, nor do we need to be guided by the worn-out model of the class struggle. Instead, we should be able to throw out as unnecessary ballast the criteria and fixed roles assigned to both sexes. We shall be able to free ourselves of our own role expectations and the expectations we have of others which have come down to us from our by-gone peasant culture.

And above all, we shall be able to free each other from the prejudices which have, unfortunately, grown all too convenient in the course of 10,000 years of patriarchy, with the different evaluation of women which has given men superiority over women. After all, we have only known since Sigmund Freud that the differentiation of sexual roles is already completed for both sexes in early childhood. This is why it could be maintained even in our own times that the completely different cultural characteristics and patterns of behavior were actually innate and natural, God-given, or at least objectively established and valid facts—whereas in fact they are developed with difficulty, if at all, by those with a lively disposition, or are avoided through illness.

Let me help us all to understand this by casting a glance back 6000 years to the cradle of our human race. Man had become a settler, and he discovered the plough. Since then his historical tool has been a masculine, male sex symbol. The land which received it was attributed to woman, the receiving one, and the domestic-emotional sphere left to her. In an after-dinner speech in 1828 Goethe put this into words: "Women are like silver dishes which we fill with golden apples."

Closer study shows that the whole sphere of sex, and the sex act itself, is by no means characterized by passive acceptance on the part of the healthy woman. Significantly enough, the act of giving birth, the "production" of the child in the so-called "expulsive state" is not included in our sexual symbolism. *Is not the father in this case the one who accepts and receives? . . .*

Among the Arapesh, a small tribe in the South Sea Islands, the child is carefully tended by both father and mother during the whole time of pregnancy. Its tiny soul can come from both father and mother; the development of the infant depends on attentive care from both parents. The mother instinct is not an innate one which is somehow released through hormones during pregnancy. The young mothers of today find it particularly difficult to learn to identify positively with their new role as one of the parents.

Polly talked about her experience:

*David, my husband and I had sorted out the role thing early in our marriage. We had to. I was an only child of middle-aged parents, and at age 25 when our first child was born, I'd never before held a baby, never a tiny baby, even though I had taught school for three years. I felt the anxiety to be a successful mother so keenly that I just couldn't cope with it and went into quite a bad postnatal depression after Sarah was born. During that year David and I grew very close, and it was at this point that we began to question our role stereotypes. David was having to do all the things which normally the mother would do, and that led us to think about what our roles were as parents rather than as mother and father.*

Jan reflected on her life as a young mother in New Zealand:

*I was 25 at that time, and our children came along very quickly, by design, and soon I had three under four years of age to take care of. It was at this point that it became very clear to me what the whole women's business was about and to my husband, too. There had to be something more to life than just the very strongly defined roles for married males and females that exist in our society. As an accountant, my husband was in a position to say, "Now you take time off every week and we'll get someone in to help. That simply has to be an expense on the household."*

*I think I would have gone mad had we not been able to make those arrangements. It's not a matter of not loving the children but simply the fact of the kind of depression that comes through confinement and sheer exhaustion. I did get to a very low ebb after the second child, and we would not want to go through that again.*

How many women have these reactions to the mother experience? 1 out of 10? 1 out of 100? There are no accurate statistics, but the growing number of postnatal depressions and child-abuse incidents indicate that there is a real basis for concern. Even if just 1 out of 100 women have an unhappy experience, that's still one million women in the United States who need to be heard.

When we discuss the relationship of women and children, we must include single women also. The nuclear family has eliminated the magnificent contribution made to the development of the child by single aunts (and uncles) who lived with the extended families of yesterday. Legislation permitting single women to adopt children ought to be the concern of all women.

Government support for children's centers where young

children can be adequately cared for while their parents (or parent) work needs to be encouraged. No child should have to suffer from lack of proper care in the absence of parents whether that absence is caused by illness, neglect, schooling, war, employment, or whatever. Proper inexpensive facilities for child care and development greatly support both parents when the stresses of modern living would otherwise make the survival of family life impossible.

Happily, many churches are using idle facilities for weekday children's programs. As government funds are withdrawn from these needs, church people can help innumerable children and their families by urging their congregational leadership to provide such programs in church buildings. The conservation of resources alone is a mighty incentive for this action, to say nothing of the opportunity to help individual women, men, and children as they struggle with the responsibilities of parenthood in our complex society.

The welfare of children all over the world is the concern of the shalom woman. Children, unwitting victims of social upheaval, must not only be cared for, but also prepared to live in a world where the rate of change is escalating with frightening speed. Mighty concern has been demonstrated by women—and largely by single women—for the children of other people.

These children include the orphans of war in Vietnam—many of them the abandoned children of American servicemen; the million or more "street children" of Latin America; the hordes of child famine victims all over our globe; and the children suffering from social inequities in our own land.

Marie of Brazil voiced her concern:

*Just recently I visited a school in the center of Sao Paulo and I was shocked to see the conditions under which the children studied. In the winter it was freezing cold, and in the summer it was so terribly hot that even the teacher couldn't stand the heat. How can children learn in such conditions? My friends who are primary-school teachers say that many times they have to buy a sandwich or something to eat for these children with their own money. Theoretically, there is a hot lunch program, but often it never is available, and the children do not have anything to eat at home before they come to school.*

To their credit, women have been willing to work for nothing or for very little in order to help child victims of injustice, but more and more they are questioning systems which produce such innocent victims. War as a way of making peace can no longer be tolerated, nor can systems which give some children a high standard of living at the expense of a majority of others. Shalom concerns itself with all children, everywhere.

### Relationships with Other Women

Learning to work together with other women is not going to be an easy task, not because women "by nature don't like to work with other women," as they've been told so often, but because they have been trained by their culture to be competitive with other women in the pursuit of men.

Without other economic opportunities available to her in the past, women and their families were in fierce competition to attract (or buy with a dowry) a man who would support her. In western society the "coming out party" and the debutante balls replaced more primitive puberty rites which announced the availability of daughters in the marriage market.

Vulnerable to attack from other men and frequently

pregnant, women have been dependent on male protection. This protection is not to be underestimated even in our country where three out of four murder victims are women and where the possibility of rape severely restricts a girl's vocational opportunities. Every girl needs to be taught techniques of self-defense in a society where rape is increasing faster than any other crime of violence.

Add to this the perspectives of a male-oriented theology and male-dominated schools of psychology which characterize women as weak, emotional, irrational, subjective, submissive, and illogical, and it's no wonder women do not want to take a chance on voting other women into positions of responsibility!

Yet an examination of the contributions women have made to history (if we take time to find the "heroines" who are largely ignored in the textbooks which glorify "heroes") gives evidence of their capabilities even in a disadvantaged cultural situation. Remember Rachel Carson whose book *Silent Spring* sparked our present ecological concern? Have you ever heard of Ida Tarbell, the journalist who spearheaded the anti-trust movement through her investigation of Standard Oil's monopoly of refineries? And how about the great Marie Curie, who won the Nobel Prize in science as a tribute to her pioneering research with radio-active materials?

Yet today, just as women fought other women to keep them from getting the vote in the early suffrage movement, women are fighting other women to keep the Equal Rights Amendment from being passed! How too bad, when what our country needs now is more female voices in political halls and in church meetings, if God's empowering "helper" is to make her influence felt.[21]

Although all women enjoy the political and economic gains made through the efforts of women's suffrage and

91

liberation movements, women's reactionary groups inevitably arise. Usually these groups rise out of church situations in which the current theology insists on the submission of women, and are largely composed of affluent married women. While loudly affirming their complete joy with housework, dishes, and large families, they heap calumny on all women's "libbers," a label reserved for anyone who even suggests a reexamination of traditional men/women roles.

Often one finds mothers of many children leading reactionary groups as though to justify themselves in defiance of growing world food shortages. Such a group met in San Francisco in November, 1974, and asserted that "there is no world population problem" and "there is no world shortage of food." [22] Two of the speakers had 18 children between them. While we cannot fault the woman who enjoys having more than the average two-point-something children, it's grotesque to make this the model for every family. Such conferences suggest a head-in-the-sand refusal to acknowledge soaring geometric population figures and threatening world famine.

Other women have organized workshops which promote a kind of "Christian sensual woman." "Use your femininity—all the traditional sex tactics—to manipulate men," is their message. The shalom woman finds such devious tricks revolting. They offer nothing to honest women, single or married, who seek ways of relating as whole persons to the men with whom they live and work.

Here again the shalom woman applauds the right of each woman to exercise her intelligent, *educated* options, and if we allow that individual preferences for several or no children are neither right nor wrong, the end result will probably be a good population balance, at least in developed countries.

The right of every woman, *wherever she lives,* to self-determination in the matter of how many children she will bear must be undergirded with adequate nutrition, sex education, health care, and equality of opportunity. In this context, U.S. women may defend with equal vigor the right of women in the Third World to have children and to protest when U.S. foreign aid is linked with birth control in underdeveloped countries. Should we impose birth control on a woman who knows that none of her babies may survive the first year of life?

Another whole area of women in relationship to other women concerns the possibility of using some women as cheap household labor so that others might be freed to advance their education and to work in the higher paying professions and occupations. Women from Third World countries readily admitted that privileged women in those countries were also tempted to do this, thus creating an oppressed class of women domestics among their own people. In order not to do this, the shalom woman who employs other women as household help must be the first to see that they are given decent wages and all the fringe benefits which she herself is struggling to attain. Shalom does not permit privileged women to take advantage of less privileged women.

Looking at the variety of relationships which women must make, one of the working groups at the consultation—a group composed of 19 women from 14 countries speaking 8 languages—developed the following definition of "partnership." It serves well as a definition of shalom relationships whether they be between women/men, women/women, and in all the areas of life where people live and work together.

"Partnership is a voluntary unit formed between two

or more people acting from a common base of respect and trust, recognizing each other's rights and conscious of each other's differences, sacrificing equally, and working together within a pattern they set for themselves toward a common goal, each contributing according to the best of his or her abilities to achieve what no one of them could have achieved alone."

As the women's movement gathers momentum, its impact will be most keenly felt in the whole area of human relationships. Pain and anger, sorrow and rage, will try to tear us apart. Healing will come when love is poured on each other's wounds. Giving and taking, asking and answering, will be demanded of each partner.

As Nelle Morton said, we will have to listen to each other's stories, "be heard and touch one another to heal and be healed."

# 6

## *Her Concerns*

At the hub of West Berlin's downtown area stand the remains of the Kaiser-Wilhelm Memorial Church, destroyed by bombs during World War II. On Wednesday afternoon of our consultation week we were free for sightseeing, and some of us went there for vesper services.

The end of the bus line was across from the church square. Standing at the bus stop and reflecting on the surroundings, I could hardly believe that bombs had once dropped destruction on this very spot. Now the Budapester Strasse with its hotels bustles by and the Tauentzien Strasse, most popular shopping street in the city, begins at this point. Here also the never-ending show of Berlin's famous highlife boulevard, the Kurfürstendamm, starts.

Yet across the street stood the wounded church steeple as a witness to the war that had once raged here.

Later, listening to the German words of the vesper

sermon, my mind wandered to the disturbing confrontation which had occurred that morning at the general session.

Mme. R. R. Andriamanjato, a civil engineer from Tananarive, Madagascar, had spoken. Her vigorous attack on the western capitalist countries and their actions toward people of the Third World had provoked a sharp debate on the floor of the assembly. Delegates had spoken to both sides of her arguments, and lunch that day was a strained affair.

The shalom of the consultation was as disrupted as Berlin in the days of the bombing.

The speaker, Chief Water Engineer for her country, teaches applied hydraulics at the University of Tananarive and was the first woman engineer in Africa. She is president of the local branch of the Malagasy Independence Congress Party and is a lay preacher of the Church of Jesus Christ of Madagascar. Condensed excerpts from the hour-long speech which she delivered in fluent French are presented here.

> Since the sadly famous Congress of Berlin in 1885 at which the Europeans divided Africa like a pie among them, the continent has lived almost entirely under the iron hand of foreigners, and even now tens of millions of men and women in Africa are living in a state of dependence. We are in the hands of people who are practicing extortion against us by exporting local products cheaply and importing goods which raise the prices in underdeveloped countries.

> In this international context of growing awareness of the realities of oppression in the world, what is the place and the role of women of Asia, Africa, and Latin America? While it depends to a

certain extent on the dominant religion or philosophical traditions, what chiefly determines it is the
social system of a country. The fact is, of course,
that in Asia, Africa, and Latin America there are
capitalist countries, colonized countries, developing countries and socialist countries.

In capitalist countries like Japan and Brazil, the
characteristic feature of women is that of "mother
of the family." If she does happen to work outside
the familiar home circle, it is because she is driven
to it by external circumstances, above all by finan-
cial and material needs. And then she is penalized
for it by being paid less for the same work men do.

In Japan women's participation in political life
is very small, and it is practically impossible for
women to attain posts of responsibility. In both
Japan and Brazil the wife is juridically a minor
and incompetent to act. In Brazil the illiteracy rate
is high—43% of women cannot read.

Women who live under colonial, racialist, or
fascist domination are subjected to double exploitation—firstly, as women, and secondly, as a result
of the exploitation under which the whole nation
suffers. The most tragic case is undoubtedly that of
women in South Africa where apartheid divides
the population and racial groups are segregated.

A paper written by a black South African woman,
Zanele Dlamini, came to us before the consultation and
spoke directly to the South African situation. Miss Dlamini, an exile from her native land, wrote that "female
oppression by Black males is the least of the Black
woman's burdens. The sexism Black women suffer most
is from the White establishment. Black male prejudices
have not dehumanized, degraded and brutalized Black

97

women to remotely the same extent that White racism and capitalist exploitation are doing. Black men are no index of equity for Black women; they do equally dreary jobs for a pittance. . . . Besides the women have been doing what is considered men's work for a very long time. Communal care of children and other dependents is probably what has helped them survive the inroads of apartheid which disrupt and threaten to destroy family life. Unrestricted birth control and abortion assume a political dimension where government policy is to reward the birth of extra White children and encourage White immigration into South Africa while it campaigns for family reduction among Blacks.

"This looks particularly sinister when the Black numbers are already reduced by acknowledged high incidents of still-births, infantile mortality rates, malnutrition, adult starvation, death sentences, and socio-political murders. From international figures it appears that South Africa accounted for nearly 50% of all legal executions in the world.

"Numbers are the only strength South Africa Blacks have in the face of a hostile government. Black women are therefore not about to campaign [by supporting birth control and abortion] for their own annihilation. . . . It is obvious that feminist issues exist in South Africa but the Black women will have to work out their own priorities according to their experience and the future society they wish to see."

Mme. Andriamanjato elaborated further on the South Africa situation.

> Cases of young coloured girls who have acquired professional training are extremely rare. The government spends ten times more on the education of white children than on that of Afri-

can children. Primary education is a luxury for black parents and secondary education even more so. The parents of African pupils, unlike those of white children, are obliged to pay school fees. In the secondary schools the mere cost of books is higher than the monthly wages of most African workers. Out of 15 million black Africans in the south, there are only 5000 university graduates.

In the French overseas territories . . . young people, chiefly girls, are taken to France and placed as domestics or maidservants. With no hope of ever being able to pay their fare back to their own country, they live a nightmare life and mostly end in prostitution.

In Mozambique which has been occupied by Portugal for 450 years women are deprived of all their rights, social, economic, and political. Subjected equally with men to forced labor, to imposed work on the land, to taxes, and ill treatment, women are also reduced by the Portuguese colonists to the humiliation of prostitution.

Even in many independent countries, polygamy is still a legal institution. In Nigeria, for instance, a husband is legally entitled to prevent his wife from obtaining a passport for traveling abroad and he is equally entitled to prevent her from getting a job.

It is mainly in agriculture that African women are at work. According to the United Nations Economic Council for Africa, 60%-80% of agricultural work in Africa is done by women, yet no vocational training in agriculture is given them; consequently, methods of cultivation remain traditional and the yield is insufficient.

Generally speaking, because of the low degree of development in these countries resulting from the grave effects of colonial domination, women have no chance of getting much schooling. Of the 80% or more Africans who are illiterate (the highest rate in the world) the great majority are women.

Mme. Andriamanjato listed one gloomy picture after another of Third World countries exploited under colonialism and impoverished by multinational corporations. For her, socialism remained the answer to sexist and racist problems in the Third World, because, as she stated, "the actual experience of countries all over the world shows us that it is only where the system that enslaves men to other men has been abolished, that equality between the sexes has been achieved."

Eva Zabolai-Csekme spoke in reply to this assertion out of her 15-year experience in Communist Hungary. "Communism," she stated emphatically, "does not automatically guarantee liberation for women!"

Helen Chung of Korea also participated in the debate following Mme. Andriamanjato's talk and in a conversation the next day made these comments:

*Oppression exists in many forms and in any society to some degree and I have witnessed the human pain and agony in the northern half of our land which is under the socialist-Communist regime. I was the only South Korean in a Red Cross delegation to have dialog with North Koreans. I found that while we in the South have a fear toward communism because of the brutal war in the early 1950s, so also do the people in the North have a terrible fear toward us. What we both found is that we were tired from the war and brutality and violence toward people under any regime. Certainly in North Korea there is no freedom of speech at all, and people cannot even move from one place to another without many, many documents.*

*Although women are working on an equal basis with men in North Korea, it's a situation where you have to work, you have no choice. If you don't work and stay home with your children, you only get a half-ration, so there you exist as a half human being. Oppression for women there is having their children taken away to a nursery school for a week or a month without choice.*

*On the other hand, I am not satisfied with the existing political power in my own country. Christ cannot be fit into one ideology no matter what system it is, and it's no use trying to replace one with the other. There is also no point of getting bitter—it's like a psychodrama where people play off their hostilities.*

Throughout the rest of that day most of the delegates from the western countries were quiet, depressed, perhaps a bit defensive. But there was no use denying, even to ourselves, that we of the U.S. are that 6% of the world's population that consumes almost 40% of its resources. We help provide a market for the diamonds and minerals mined through the toil of South African blacks—underpaid, separated from their families, and cruelly restricted in their freedoms. The very multinational corporations which exploit humans in the underdeveloped countries also provide us with the material goods which we have come to expect as our right.

While shalom does also mean "well-being"—and that well-being is not just in the sense of spirit or happiness, but the emphasis of the Hebrew is on the material side, enough to eat, health, and all the other things we consider material blessings—it cannot exist for some at the expense of others! The shalom well-being almost always has a collective sense. To maintain our standard of living, our "American way of life," at the expense of the impoverished people of the world brings us under judgment. That judgment is clear from the words of 1 Cor.

101

6:10 where the Scriptures tell us that the "greedy" will not inherit the kingdom of God.

Here then is the reason why women from around the world need to come together. As we listen to each other's stories, we begin to see the problems of the world from a human point of view and not only from the perspective of business or politics. Hopefully, as more women get into positions of influence, this point of view will modify some of the decisions that are responsible for much human misery in other parts of the world.

It was a young Rhodesian woman who brought healing to the consultation the next day. She asked for permission at one of the general sessions to read a letter, explaining that whenever she faced a puzzling situation in her life, she tried to work it out by writing a letter to God.

*West Berlin,*
*21st June, 1974*

*Dear Lord,*

*Another of those letters, Lord.*

*Let me start by thanking you for this opportunity for the company and fellowship of so many women. And for the variety, and diversity—cultural, racial and the rest.*

*But we have had to pay the price of such a rich diversity in various forms of misunderstanding—the main among them being our different languages. We have all had a test of the tower of Babel.*

*The price of being hurt because I think they do not understand what I am trying to communicate, because I get sympathy instead of empathy.*

*Others have been hurt because they have been called oppressors. They are human beings too. They feel. But maybe we forget that most of us who are here are op-*

102

*pressors because we belong to the privileged classes of our nations.*

*Yes, Lord, we have had to pay the price of the richness of coming together. But I hope, Lord, that we will realize that whatever way we felt, we have learned that working together for liberation—that reconciliation—is a painful process. It requires that we be open, frank, and honest with each other. This is where being Christians, for me, makes the difference between our groups here and the United Nations. Because whatever we do should be done in perfect love which casts away all those fears and prejudices in us.*

*And this talk of liberation, Lord, is confusing because it means different things to different people. For me and my people in Southern Africa, it means to be human for a dehumanized people—not that I don't want women's liberation, but that I am not yet human.*

*For my friend from England it means to be more than just being a wife and mother. For the Palestinian refugee it means having a place to call home.*

*But I suppose, Lord, that what this consultation has been about is to share and to help each other find out how we as women can effectively work for the liberation of the whole society.*

*I wish I had more time, Lord, I would elaborate. But that is one thing we do not have here—time, time to elaborate all those things that we have misunderstood.*

*Yours,*

*Olivia Nyembezi Mukuna*

Olivia's words were a litany of confession and absolution, and Annie Jiagge, wise Justice from Ghana, sensed the need of a response from the delegates. She moved to a microphone and said, "Salvation will not

103

come from another ideology. We are all Christians and we have our ideology."

That afternoon at a press conference a journalist asked the pointed question, "To what extent does the rest of the conference support Mme. Andriamanjato and her views?"

Justice Jiagge again replied, "For myself I only subscribe to the gospel of Jesus Christ. If we develop an ideology in Africa, it will have to come out of our own experience. It is very difficult to get a group like this to support only one political ideology, but we can all support the ideology of Christ."

So we tacitly agreed to disagree about our political views and instead to look together at the causes of injustice and what could be done about them.

One thing is certain. Women—and above all church women—in the U.S. must become better informed about the condition of other women on our globe. To live as though the rest of the world enjoys all the privileges which we take for granted as our human rights is inexcusable.

God calls us now to account for the stewardship of our lives and goods. When many women have not even potable water, to say nothing of food, available for their families, then there is no shalom for us either.

### Women in the U.S.

For U.S. women another question asks for a hearing at this point. Can—*will*—our country *voluntarily* right some of the injustices under which women suffer here, or will only political change accomplish this? Given the will to do it, can we change ourselves?

When a reporter asked Annie Jiagge this question, "What can men hope to gain through better representation for women in the church?" she answered, "We hope that men will come to realize that a woman's problem is a man's problem. We have the same problems in life but look at them from another point of view. *Just give us a chance and see if we will not have a better world!"*

Give us a chance!

We still have time to change ourselves, but change we must. Justice for women demands it. It's appalling that women have no representative of their own sex in the U.S. Senate and no woman to speak their cause as a justice on the Supreme Court. How can women work for shalom wholeness here or anywhere else without representation or voice?

As one of the first steps toward self-change, passage of the Equal Rights Amendment is imperative for establishing equality for women on a solid basis. Although first introduced in Congress in 1923, this amendment was held in the House Judiciary Committee for 47 years! It cannot wait any longer.

Writing in *Judicature*, Doris L. Sassower, a New York attorney, says that the ERA will put an end to "traditional practices and judicial interpretations which have perpetuated a subordinate role for women." [23] But long before an Equal Rights Amendment was introduced, she says, "the judiciary defined the rights of women. Women's inequality in society has been reinforced by courts constituted so as to be unrepresentative of women and unresponsive to their needs." [24]

The unequal rights of women stem mainly from a basic legal assumption that women are not persons under our Constitution. As legal inferiors they have been denied rights given to men under that same Constitution. Articulated most definitively in *Bradwell v. Illinois* in 1873, that case was one of the first used by the U.S.

Supreme Court to uphold the constitutionality of state laws discriminating against women.

Mr. Justice Bradley of the Supreme Court gave the concurring opinion which supported the Illinois Court's denial of Myra Bradwell's application for a license to practice law with these all-inclusive words:

> It certainly cannot be affirmed, as an historical fact, that this [the right to pursue any lawful occupation] has ever been established as one of the fundamental privileges and immunities of the sex. On the contrary, the civil law, as well as nature herself, has always recognized a wide difference in the respective spheres and destinies of man and woman. Man is, or should be, woman's protector and defender. The natural and proper timidity and delicacy which belongs to the female sex evidently unfits it for many of the occupations of civil life. . . . The paramount destiny and mission of woman are to fulfill the noble and benign offices of wife and mother. This is the law of the Creator.[25]

Although the "law of the Creator" has no documentation other than that which exists in male-dominated courts and unions, it has been used through the years to launch all sorts of "protective" legislation which succeeds also in keeping women from the higher paying job categories.

A substantial increase in the number of women lawyers and judges is needed to enable women to influence judicial processes in support of those causes which they see as important. In 1969, states Attorney Sassower, there were not many more than 8,000 women lawyers and fewer than 200 of the 10,000 judges in the U.S. were women, and the majority of these were in the lower courts. The American Bar Association has released

106

figures which show more than 12,000 women attending law school in 1972-73, seven times more than there were ten years ago, and more than double the number in 1970. The 5000 first-year women law students in 1974 represent an increase of 27 percent over two years ago. These are encouraging signs.

"Something new, too, are feminist law firms, formed by women for the specific purpose of undertaking sex discrimination cases, and which give women a kind of representation they have sorely lacked in the past," says Ms. Sassower.

It's unbelievable that President Nixon who had four opportunities to appoint new justices to the Supreme Court, should never have selected a woman as one of them! The fact that so few women can be found who "qualify" is due to the fact that federal and state executives continually pass over women in the appointment of judgeships. Florence Allen is the only woman ever to have attained a chief judgeship of a United States circuit court and, in her autobiography *To Do Justly,* she tells how on account of her sex she was not even able to gain acceptance from her junior colleagues.[26]

With larger numbers of women entering the legal professions and with women uniting as a political force, some of the inequities militating against them in our society may disappear.

Some of these inequities appear in the large disparities between the income levels of women and men in all areas of employment. The Equal Pay Act of 1963 and the Civil Rights Acts of 1964 are legislative efforts to equalize the pay differences between men and women, but many women do not press their rights in employment situations for fear of reprisals.

Since 1948, the number of women, aged 20 and over, in the labor force has increased by 91% while the num-

107

ber of men has risen only 20%. With women representing approximately 40% of the labor force now, they are a number to be reckoned with. If this were just a matter of women working for "pin money" or out of sheer boredom, we might seek alternatives for them, but we are dealing with a rapidly increasing number of women who are heads of households. Yet, in the year 1971, full-time working women who headed families were earning almost 40% less than male family heads. At that time, these women had a median income of $6168 which is certainly not sufficient for adequately housing, feeding, and clothing a single woman, to say nothing of one who has children to support.

Where did we get the notion that the work women do deserves less pay than the work men do? It all goes back again to theological and cultural ideas that women are second-rate human beings and therefore any work they engage in must be inferior work. Even in clerical jobs where more than one-third of working women are employed, their median income is 36% less than that of male clerical workers. Women employed as managers earn just a little more than half of the income of male managers for the same work, yet men in this occupational group have the highest median income.

Since women receive no discounts at grocery stores, gas stations, or rent deductions because they are women, justice demands that they also receive equal pay for their work.[27]

If the situation of women church staff workers were investigated under current legislation seeking to better the conditions of employed women, the church would fare badly.

When church secretaries in the United Presbyterian Church USA returned 2488 questionnaires inquiring about their working conditions, the following results were tabulated:

- — 37% were over 50 years old
- — 85% were not on any private pension plan
- — 35% were not having any church funds paid into the government social security system for them (in many cases this was probably illegal on the part of the church)
- — 11% only indicated that the church provided access to medical plan coverage
- — 25% received no paid vacation
- — 50% of the full-time (40 hours a week) and nearly all of the part-time (though some work 30-35 hours) receive less than $5,000 a year (welfare family level in the U.S.).[28]

While the problems of the single woman who must support herself against such odds are bad enough, the plight of the divorced or widowed woman is often even more disheartening.

Jokes of male comedians about the hardships alimony works on men to the contrary, women suffer more from divorce than men do in the U.S. Even though the Roper poll indicated that women prefer marriage as a way of life, one out of three marriages ends in divorce. Currently, "more than half the divorces granted are instigated by husbands. Husbands instigate the overwhelming number of divorces over forty. Desertion, the 'poor man's divorce' does not show up in the statistics." [29]

While divorce is a traumatic experience for one or both mates whenever it occurs, it is especially hard on the older woman or the woman with children. Looking at this situation, Clare Boothe Luce writes, "If the marriage ends in divorce, the wife must go to work to support herself, or she must depend either on her ex-husband's charity or on the charity of the courts. This charitable handout is called alimony. Permanent alimony is awarded in only 2 percent of all divorces, and the average alimony award is less than 30 percent of the ex-husband's wages. In awarding child support, the majority of judges generally expect able-bodied women to go to work and to assume half the cost of supporting their children." [30]

When a woman who has not been employed for several years tries to reenter the competitive job market against younger women, she finds herself in a most difficult situation. Her self-confidence has been struck a vital blow by the divorce; her job skills are rusty or non-existent; she must pay for child care. The woman who has stayed professionally active while married is in a much more tenable position should a divorce occur in the middle years.

If it were not for their economic vulnerability, perhaps more women would initiate divorce proceedings. They hesitate to complain because they know their husband holds the upper hand by being able to support himself without her. They know also that "uppity" wives can be divorced and replaced by younger and more submissive ones.

Coupled with her economic dilemma, most divorced women find themselves regarded with suspicion by their married sisters. Somehow, other women seem to lay the failure of the marriage to her account even when her husband gets the divorce and marries that younger woman. Why wasn't she able to "hold him"? Did she nag him? Did she run around doing too much outside of the home?

Speaking to this issue at the consultation, a French woman lawyer said that although the law in France requires both men and women to show guilt in getting a divorce, attitudes affecting the judge's decisions differ. It is accepted as being normal, for instance, for a man to spend at least half of his time away from the home, whereas women are not given that same opportunity. This was demonstrated in the case of a policeman who killed his wife because he could not accept her activities in labor unions and in other liberation causes. The court ruled the case to be dismissed because "her activities provoked him."

Younger men and women tend to pick themselves up and go on living after a divorce, especially where children are not involved. But for divorced or deserted women with children and for older divorced women, the understanding and help of other women is vital to their continued existence.

Because women have less earning power throughout their lifetime and usually abandon their careers when they marry, old age is a particular burden for them. In fact, the problems of the aged in the U.S. are largely a woman's problem.

Women live longer than men; they are the inhabitants of old people's homes; they are the widows who live alone. Because the average woman marries a man who is three years older than herself and her life expectancy is seven years more than his, she can anticipate spending the last ten years of her life alone.

Since she usually has not been employed outside the home during her marriage (only 30 million of 80 million adult women in the U.S. are gainfully employed), she faces some inequities in social security benefits. Add to that the fact that her husband's pension may cease with his death, and one begins to see what makes these women one of the largest poverty groups in our land.

111

Every caring husband needs to question his company's pension policies and its provisions for his wife, since he is likely to precede her in death. While there is some hesitancy in talking about these matters, the wife herself ought to be informed about them early if she is to stay at home during the marriage and forsake her own career. Her future is at stake. Since the productivity of a man in his career depends on his having a wife who runs his home and takes care of their children, it is obviously grossly unjust for companies to cut off his pension just when she needs it most.

After age 65 a woman faces a very depressing set of statistics. Before that it may be more stressful to be a man, but after that "a statistical flip-flop occurs. There are more women than men in mental hospitals, and after 65 the percentage escalates dramatically. Our nursing-home population is 80% female," reports Shana Alexander.[31] She asked Dr. Robert Butler, a psychiatric authority on aging and a consultant to the U.S. Senate Special Committee on Aging, why this was so.

"Mainly because most men over 65 have a living wife. Most women end up taking care of a dying husband. She's 63 when he dies. Twenty years later she's 83; economic erosion has eaten up 30 or 40 percent of her capital; she's probably used the rest to help pay for her son's heart attack and her grandchildren's education. Some people say it's her fault that she didn't manage or invest more wisely, but society never taught her to manage money. If her son dies, her daughter-in-law may not take her in, not necessarily through malevolence but perhaps because she herself has remarried."

It is not enough to enable people, especially women, to live longer, unless they are prepared to live productively for a longer time after their children are grown and their husband is gone. Ms. Alexander points to the

112

fact that, although people over 65 now constitute over 10% of our population, there is not a single university or medical-school chair of geriatric medicine in what she labels "Kids' Country." At this time, less than 3% of National Institute of Mental Health funds are being spent on the problems of the aging.

To help women plan for a productive lengthened life span, attempts are being made in the Federal Republic of Germany to promote the idea of life planning. Frau Irmgard Bohm, president of the Family Education Center and a member of the board of the International Council of Women said that families are being encouraged and educated to help their daughters with "life planning" very early, so they will be prepared for independent existence.

Whether it be in global or local concerns, women must begin to see themselves as agents of change. The potential of women as creative innovators is unlimited, if they ever catch on to their own creative ability. Women have incredible amounts of work energy and management ability, a fact that is evidenced in every women's organization and in every volunteer activity they undertake.

But just to keep on binding up the wounds caused by injustice and misfortune is not enough. In addition to this, women must band together to change the systems which are creating those hurts and making the wounds.

Olivia, in her letter, asked for empathy instead of sympathy. Sympathy comforts the miserable; empathy works to correct the causes of their misery. Jesus said his agenda was to "set at liberty those who are oppressed" (Luke 4:18), not just to comfort them in their oppression.

The shalom woman, living out this ideology of Jesus Christ, repeats Annie Jiagge's words and works to make them come true: "Just give us a chance and see if we will not have a better world!"

*7*

# *Her Hopes*

On Thursday night we celebrated.

After that evening's session we walked through the rain to another building where a party had been prepared for us. All the delights of the German cuisine were there—the sausages, the cheese, the good breads, and the other delightful things that give German hospitality its reputation. Candles and music gave the setting a sense of intimacy.

We had worked through concepts and conflicts, and the week was almost over. Work groups still had to piece together their reports, and deadlines were pressing. But that night we celebrated, and in the celebration came to know each other in new ways.

If only there were more opportunities for people of differing races and cultural backgrounds to dance their dances and sing their songs for one another and to be children together, there might be less of war and opposing forces and more of understanding and loving.

Anna Gultom, the principal of a teachers' training school in Sumatra, and Shanti Zechariah, the labor union organizer from Malaysia, performed a Malaysian dance for us. In the whirling silken sheen of sari and kabaya we saw some of the laughter and fun of the Indonesian people. Watching Shanti dance, it was easy to see why the women among whom she worked could respond to her dreams for them. She must radiate among them like a star of hope.

*The role of the migrant Indian woman on the rubber estate is very fascinating and very complex. She wakes up in the morning, possibly the first one to waken, at four o'clock, because she has to provide for the family before she goes out to work. So she makes three little packages, one for herself and her husband to take away, a second package to leave at home for the children who come home from school, and a third package to take to the day nursery which will look after her babies while she is gone. So she has to do all this before appearing at roll call, or muster, before six in the morning on the rubber plantation because the best flow of quality latex comes in the morning. It's imperative that she work as a "tapper" of the rubber trees because she must supplement the family budget if they are going to live.*

*At ten o'clock in the morning she comes back, picks up the babies from the nursery, brings them home and now must forget about the hard work on the plantation and be wholly devoted to mothering. In the afternoon she becomes the laundress because she must wash the dirty clothes from the nursery so they are ready again the next morning. She might have a little bit of leisure between three and four, but then she must hurry to cook the night meal which is the main meal of the day when her husband comes home. After the washing up of the dishes and the evening care of the children, she must*

115

become the desirable wife that her husband wants her to be.

She has so much to do in her complex life that you can't expect her to know even what day of the week it is, but just to survive. She goes by two or three major incidents in her life; one is payday because then the rice pot is full and the whole family is being well fed. The second one is rather amusingly, her menstruation cycle because then her husband won't look at another woman while she can still bear children. So by these incidents she spends her entire life.

I would like to change her—to make her feel again. This indifference, this mind that has gone to sleep—the tragedy is that she has lost hope. She thinks, I am just an Indian, a migrant, this is my fate, this is my life. No aspirations, no thinking. My dream, my hope, what I would like to do is to reawaken both the woman and the man to think of themselves as completely human. The Asian woman is very strong, very effective. All she needs is hope.

I could believe this, watching tiny, gentle Anna dance with her, and remembering that Anna had told me that she usually *walked* to make the rounds of the 129 schools under her supervision!

When the women from South America joined hands to present a Brazilian dance, one began to understand the importance of music and dance to people who live with constant hunger and poverty. One's spiritual survival may depend on that. Marie, Japanese but with her "future and destiny" linked to Brazil's, watched them from the shadows. I wondered if she remembered what she had told me.

Of course I am realistic enough to know that political and economic liberation will not automatically bring liberation to women in our country, because the feudal-

116

*istic orientation places women in an inferior position while men in Brazil can do pretty much anything they want. But many girls from the upper and middle classes are attending universities and studying medicine and engineering and preparing for any field they choose. But I can only hope that in our country when you speak about the liberation of women that we talk first of all about liberation from economic needs—simply to have at least a human life, to have adequate food, proper clothing, health, housing and at least the basic education. When we can cooperate on those things then we will have at least the beginnings of liberation.*

In another mood, Dr. Anima Bose, university professor from Bombay University, sang of the longings of her ancient people in the words of a song by Rabindranath Tagore. We felt the universality of its minor strains.

But the festive spell could not be broken for long, and when the Korean women went down on hands and knees to touch their foreheads to the floor three times in demonstration of the sexist bow Korean brides must perform after the wedding ceremony to show complete obedient servitude to their husbands, there were a few unladylike hisses with the applause! I remembered one of the performers telling us in a group session about the horrors of tourist promotion in Korea with young Korean virgins used as the bait to attract male tourists, especially from Japan. In the discussion that followed that day, it was agreed that the world-wide prostitution which enslaves young, economically-depressed women may be one of the most hopeless situations for women in any day.

Two quite dignified women—church workers from England and Scotland—paired in a Scottish dance, "The Gay Gordons," done to recorded bagpipes and live hand-clapping. Polly Haslam watched with delight and the

117

memory of her crisp Oxford syllables came to my mind.

*I just hope that some of the power that I've been given this week will still be there when we move to London in a couple of months. I feel that I have lots of things to shout about and I want to go home and shout about them. I wish David could have been here to share the feelings that I've had, but it's also come to me that maybe this week is very much just for women and some of the things we will be able to communicate to our men when we get home and some other things we'll want to keep to ponder inside ourselves. Maybe that's where our strength will come from.*

When the women from South Africa sang their song in the Xosa language, it echoed all the songs sung by prisoners through the centuries, including Paul and Silas. Pointing out the need to liberate all people, male-female, a woman from Uruguay said, "In prison there is true equality. The same pain is suffered by men and women alike."

In between the songs and dances, intimate dreams and hopes were shared. Liebje, the journalist from Holland, talked about her children.

*We have made them sensitive. From very young we have pointed them to the feelings of people, and when they are eighteen they still have this sensitivity. Maybe it's a good thing but the burden they're under is great, and sometimes I envy the women we see here who have so much still to work for. The industrial nation has no inspiration for us any more. There's nothing to reach to. You love your things instead of warmth, and we're sold on that idea all the time—if you buy things you get warmth. What we need is to develop the warmth again and drop the things. If we didn't have so many things to distract us, maybe we would return to old time Christian values like being sober and having companionship and*

118

*reading the Bible again. It's not possible to just turn the clock back. I can't take the sensitiveness out of my children and make them hard again, but maybe we can find new ways to friendship and companionship. It's something I long for very much.*

People have to be seen as single units and not as collective groups if their lives are to have any meaning for others. To lump them all together as "the aged" or "the blacks" removes them from the possibility of relationship. The death of one million people can mean very little, but the death of one person is significant.

When Anaseini Qionibaravi, the Senator from the Fiji Islands, led us all in a pantomime of the nursery rhyme "Four-and-Twenty Blackbirds Baked in a Pie," it was almost with a sense of shock that we realized that just about every woman there had taught that song to her children with exactly the same words and movements!

What are we going to do without our old familiar stereotypes to fall back upon for easy reference? Anaseini has changed forever my image of a Polynesian woman living in the Fiji Islands!

Perhaps Liebje's longing for a world where there was something "to work for" is being realized by those women in the new countries of the Third World. We are industrialized; we are developed. Where does the road ahead lead?

For Tamo Diro of Papua New Guinea, the road ahead is exciting.

*Women have a long way to go in Papua New Guinea, but since our first woman university graduate in 1968, many more are coming along very fast. But because women are unable to overcome the traditional male dominance of public life, political participation of women has been very slow. It's only in the last two years that women chose to enter the elections for parliament. Al-*

119

*though they've been much organized through voluntary women's societies to mobilize electoral support, men fail to recognize the political strengths and abilities of women.*

*This is one area where I'm working very hard to help women see that they must infiltrate if they are going to make any impact at all on the society and status of women in our community. But it's exciting to live in Papua New Guinea now. We're going through some exciting stages of development and have only been a self-governing country for six months. It's a young men's and young women's country with many of our leaders in their thirties and forties and only a few in their fifties. Give the women of Papua New Guinea another five years, and you will hear more exciting and interesting roles played by women for the creation of a new nation.*

Another kind of celebration came on Saturday morning when we gathered around the communion table in an Agape Feast. In the eating of the bread and the drinking of the wine, the death of our Lord was once more experienced with its message of forgiveness. Only by that miracle of grace will women be able to forgive the writers of the histories that have ignored them, the political leaders of systems that have degraded them, and the ecclesiastical hierarchies that have repressed them.

While forgiveness must be permitted to bring its shalom into our lives, the shalom woman cannot do those whom she forgives the disservice of allowing them to remain in anti-shalom positions. While she loves and forgives the ones who sin against her, she can no longer permit the sins of sexism (and racism) to continue wherever it becomes identified. God's grace will also give her strength to fight that sin.

The messianic hope of shalom beckons. Isaiah pictures a time when the "wolf shall dwell with the lamb, and

120

the leopard shall lie down with the kid" (Isa. 11:6), and when "the earth shall be full of the knowledge of the Lord as the waters cover the sea."

According to the Old Testament prophets, the Messiah would usher in that shalom day. It's time for the church to lead society into it. It's no longer sufficient to keep on saying the words of liberation and acceptance, to pass the right policy statements and to say aye to the right resolutions. *The important thing is to start demonstrating in its behavior the wholeness of the Body of Christ.*

The shalom woman will continue to work for that day to come. Hers is no esoteric cause; it concerns at least half of the people on this earth. If it were not sweeping across the globe in such inclusive proportions, she might doubt her own concern for wholeness.

Oppression has done the damage; liberation in and through the gospel can only heal. Alienation may precede reconciliation, but shalom for some is intolerable if it is at the expense of others. The force of liberation as a world-wide movement permits no turning back. The eschatological hope of the shalom woman is no less than a world in which the Prince of Shalom rules.

The rain was still falling when the taxi came on Saturday morning to take us to the airport. The words and melody of a song sung during the communion service hung hauntingly in the memory during the silent ride.

> One woman's hands can't tear a prison down,
> Two women's hands can't tear a prison down,
> But if two and two make fifty make a million,
> We'll see that day come 'round,
> We'll see that day come 'round.

In that taxi were a woman from Nigeria, another from Lebanon, and one from the United States. They

121

would probably never meet again, but they were still part of a global community. The words of Mary Tulip, a teacher from Epping, Australia, would make a fitting farewell for them.

> We have a new community to help us—a healing, supporting community, a community of liberation, a new sisterhood. As we are able to believe in ourselves, to trust each other as women, and to share our deepest experiences—our hurt, our horror, and our joy—we are no longer separated by race, or class, or by our sense of lack of worth. In creating a new community of acceptance and wholeness, we are on the way to creating a new world.

Shalom.

# NOTES

1. C. G. Jung, *Modern Man in Search of a Soul* (New York: Harcourt, Brace, 1966) p. 197.
2. Johs. Pedersen, *Israel, Its Life and Culture* (London: Oxford University Press, 1926) p. 263.
3. Jung, p. 197.
4. Jung, p. 197.
5. Jung, p. 198.
6. Mary Daly, *The Church and the Second Sex* (New York: Harper & Row, 1968) p. 49.
7. J. Edgar Bruns, *God as Woman, Woman as God* (New York: Paulist Press, 1973) pp. 36-37.
8. Richard Wurmbrand, *Stronger Than Prison Walls* (New Jersey: Fleming Revell, 1969) pp. 33-34.
9. Wurmbrand, p. 34.
10. Bruns, p. 40.
11. *Los Angeles Times* (Mar. 23, 1974) Pt. I, pp. 1, 5.
12. For a comprehensive study of the Inquisition and its persecution of women especially see Nancy Van Vuuren, *The Subversion of Women as Practiced by Churches, Witch-hunters, and Other Sexists* (Philadelphia: Westminster Press, 1973).
13. Russell C. Prohl, *Women in the Church* (Grand Rapids: Eerdmans, 1957) p. 70.
14. Prohl, p. 80.
15. Prohl, p. 80.
16. *Church Employed Women Newsletter,* Carol Ames, ed. (Published by Church Employed Women, an organization related to the United Presbyterian Church in the USA, Box 427, Forest Grove, Pa. 18922) Material prepared by Joyce L. Manson.
17. Susan Copenhaver Barrabee, "Education for Liberation: Women in the Seminary," *Women's Liberation and the Church,* ed. Sarah Bentley Doely (New York: Association Press, 1970) p. 59.
18. Merton P. Strommen, Milo L. Brekke, Ralph C. Underwager, Arthur L. Johnson, *A Study of Generations*

Minneapolis: Augsburg Publishing House, 1972) pp. 267-268.

19. Pedersen, p. 309.

20. *Los Angeles Times*, (Oct. 6, 1975) Pt. IX, pp. 1, 14.

21. Prohl, p. 37: In Genesis 2:18 we read, "The Lord God said: It is not good for man to be alone, I will make him an help meet for him." The key words, according to Pieper, are "help" and "meet," in the Hebrew, *ezer* and *neged*. The preposition *neged* is translated as "before," "in the presence of," "in the sight of." For example, in Psalm 16:8 we read, "I have set the Lord always *before* me." The noun *ezer* means "help" or "helper." It is used twenty-one times in the Old Testament, and sixteen times it is used for a superordinate, not a subordinate, helper. In no case is the one who helps subordinate unless we consider Genesis 2:18, 20 as exceptions. The most common use of *ezer* is in reference to Jehovah as a help. In Psalm 33:20 we read: "The Lord, He is our help." Exodus 18:4, "For the God of my father was my help." If this word *ezer*, "help," does indicate a grade or rank, we should conclude from its use elsewhere in the Old Testament that Adam was subordinate to Eve. The truth is that the word itself indicates neither a higher nor a lower grade or rank.

22. *Orange County Evening News* (Garden Grove, Calif., Nov. 9, 1974) p. 105.

23. Doris L. Sassower, "Women and the Judiciary: Undoing 'The Law of the Creator,'" *Judicature* (Chicago: American Judicature Society, Vol. 57, Number 7, Feb., 1974) p. 285.

24. Sassower, p. 283.

25. Sassower, p. 283.

26. Sassower, p. 287.

27. Sources of this information are from the Bureau of the Census and the Bureau of Labor Statistics.

28. *Church Employed Women Newsletter*.

29. Clare Boothe Luce, "Women: A Technological Castaway," *The Saturday Evening Post* (Indianapolis: January/February, 1974) p. 18.

30. Luce, p. 18.

31. Shana Alexander, "Getting Old in Kids' Country," *Newsweek* (New York: November 11, 1974) p. 124.

# FOR FURTHER READING

Armstrong, Frieda, *To Be Free* (Philadelphia: Fortress Press, 1974).
Especially good for teen-agers.

Bardwick, Judith M., *Psychology of Women* (New York: Harper & Row, 1971).
An excellent study of bio-cultural conflicts, responsibly integrated biological, psychological and medical data.

Bird, Caroline, *Born Female* (New York: David McKay, 1968).
The social, moral and personal costs of limiting woman's role to the home.

Bruns, J. Edgar, *God as Woman, Woman as God* (New York: Paulist Press, 1973).
Introduction to views of women in early religious thought.

Cade, Toni, ed., *The Black Woman* (Signet, 1970).
Articulate black women speak out.

Callahan, Sidney Cornelia, *The Working Mother* (New York: Macmillan, 1971).
Sixteen women tell how they successfully combine careers and childbearing.

Collins, Sheila, *A Different Heaven and Earth* (Valley Forge: Judson Press, 1974).
A good introduction to feminist theologizing in the United States.

Daly, Mary, *The Church and the Second Sex* (New York. Harper & Row, 1968).
An exploration of the historical and theological oppression of women by the church.

Doely, Sarah Bentley, ed., *Women's Liberation and the Church* (New York: Association Press, 1970).
Excellent anthology exploring the demands for freedom by women of the church with a projection of its impact on the church's future.

Ermarth, Margaret Sittler, *Adam's Fractured Rib* (Philadelphia: Fortress, 1970).
Special attention to women in specific denominations in the U.S. and abroad. Grew out of a Lutheran study into the role of women in the church.

125

Flexner, Eleanor, *Century of Struggle: The Women's Rights Movement in the U.S.* (New York: Atheneum, 1968).
The major scholarly history.

Friedan, Betty, *The Feminine Mystique* (New York: Dell, 1963).
Still the classical documentation of the forces which have worked to limit the options of women in the U.S.

Graebner, Alan, *After Eve: The New Feminism* (Minneapolis: Augsburg, 1972).
An introduction to the women's movement with a study guide.

Hewitt, Emily and Hiatt, Susan, *Women Priests: Yes or No?* (New York: Seabury, 1973).
A sharp, humorous clarification of those factors which make full acceptance of women ministers difficult. Written for the debate on women's ordination in the Episcopal Church in the U.S.

Hobbs, Lisa, *Love and Liberation* (New York: McGraw-Hill, 1970).
A hopeful analysis of the humanizing changes being brought by the "new woman."

Janeway, Elizabeth, *Man's World: Woman's Place* (New York: Morrow, 1971).
Study of the meaning of myths about women in our time and their effect on roles.

Maccoby, Eleanor F., *Development of Sex Differences* (Stanford, 1966).
An extensive summary of psychological data comparing males and females.

Russell, Letty, *Ferment of Freedom* (New York: YWCA, 1973).
Good study book for women's groups working through ideas about liberation.

Russell, Letty, *Human Liberation in a Feminist Perspective* (Philadelphia: Westminster, 1974).
Thorough discussion of liberation theology in relationship to women.

Stendahl, Krister, *The Bible and the Role of Women* (Philadelphia: Fortress, 1966).
A look at the historical and hermeneutical relationships affecting women's role in the church.

Swidler, Arlene Anderson, *Woman in a Man's Church: From Role to Person* (New York: Paulist Press, 1973).

Small volume exploring the many facets of women's experiences in a male-dominated church.

United Methodist Church, Board of Missions, *New World Outlook* (LXI:4, April, 1971).

Entire issue on "Third World Women" with articles expressing an awareness that women throughout the world can shape their future.

van Vuuren, Nancy, *The Subversion of Women as Practiced by Churches, Witch-hunters, and Other Sexists* (Philadelphia: Westminster Press, 1973).

An analysis of the effect historical oppression has had on the attitudes and behavior of women.

# ACKNOWLEDGMENTS

Permission to quote freely from speech texts and written materials which were part of the Consultation, *Sexism in the Nineteen-Seventies: Discrimination Against Women,* has been granted by Ms. Frances Smith of the Department of ⸻ the World Council of Churches in Ge⸻.

⸻ ⸻ from women participants at the consultation were taped with their knowledge and used with their permission. The author wishes to thank these women for their willingness to share in this way their thoughts, their feelings and the events of their lives with women in the United States.

We are also grateful to the following publishers and authors for permission to quote from their publications:

William B. Eerdmans Publishing Co., Grand Rapids, Mich., for Russell Prohl, *Woman in the Church,* 1957.

The American Judicature Society for Doris L. Sassower, "Women Look at Justice in America" (*Judicature,* February, 1974).

The Paulist Press, New Jersey, for J. Edgar Bruns, *God as Woman, Woman as God,* 1973.

Association Press, New York, for Susan Copenhaver Barrabee's "Education for Liberation: Women in the Seminary," in *Women's Liberation and the Church,* Sarah Bentley Doely, ed., 1970.

Harcourt, Brace and Jovanovich, Inc., New York, for C. G. Jung, *Modern Man in Search of a Soul,* 1933.

Richard Wurmbrand, *Stronger Than Prison Walls,* (New Jersey: Fleming H. Revell Co., 1969).

Shana Alexander, "Getting Old in Kids' Country," (*Newsweek,* Nov. 11, 1974).

*1973 Britannica Book of the Year,* copyright 1973, Encyclopedia Britannica, Inc., Chicago, Illinois, for Clare Booth Luce, "Woman: A Technological Castaway."

# The Shalom Woman

## USING THIS STUDY GUIDE

The Shalom Woman is written in the style of a
journey that involves the author and many others who
are undergoing changes in their consciousness of what
it means to be women and men.  The reader is invited to
participate in that journey.  You might do that:
>    1) individually, using this study guide to help
>       focus the issues for your own life; or
>    2) in a small group of 4-12 persons.

If a group is specifically gathered for this study
it might be composed of women whose needs or interests
are not being met by existing organizations, women who
are seeking change in the church and/or their own lives,
or women who are just beginning to question some of the
usual assumptions made about women and men.  If men are
included, realize that the dynamics and perhaps the per-

Prepared under the auspices of the Division for Life and Mission in the Con-
gregation and the Board of Publication of the American Lutheran Church.  This
study guide, by Karen Bloomquist, is to be used with the book "The Shalom
Woman" by Margaret Wold, Augsburg, ISBN 0-8066-1475-7.  Study guide © 1975
Augsburg Publishing House.  Additional copies for 10¢ each, $1.10 dozen from
Augsburg Publishing House, 426 S. Fifth St., Minneapolis, Minnesota  55415.

sonal sharing will be significantly affected. A men's group might want to discuss the book on their own.

It is intended that personal sharing be central in the discussion of the book. Therefore, plan a minimum of seven 1-1/2 or 2 hour sessions.

One "facilitator" could lead all the sessions, or that function could rotate among the members. If the group is composed of women, it should be led by a woman. The "facilitator" can decide beforehand which of the questions would be most beneficial to consider.


# CHAPTER 1: HER COMMON JOURNEY

If your group is newly formed, invite each member to share: What has been good and what not-so-good about being female or male? How have you changed through the years? What are your concerns today? This is your take-off point! You might want to contrast your past "journey" with the author's. Be aware of how the re-claiming of your personal history involves a moving toward "the sunrise of new knowledge" (p. 7).

Then consider together:

1. Does the prospect of new possibilities give you a sense of excitement and adventure? Of fear of the unknown? Of wanting to hang on to the past?

2. What do you consider to be the scope of women's concerns?

3. What is the difference in thinking of "freedom in Christ" as a journey rather than as a destination (p. 7)?

4. Discuss the concept of shalom. What is its function in relation to the walls of separation? Consult a Bible dictionary or commentary.

5. Her search for wholeness takes the author over the waters, through the darkness. What "waters" and "darkness" have been a part of your journey?

6. Notice the diversity of concerns on pp. 10-19. Try to identify with at least one of these women. What does it feel like to share her cares, concerns, pains?


# CHAPTER 2: HER AWAKENING

1. Discuss your reactions to Soromundi (p. 21). What about it bothers or excites you?

2. Why does Dr. Potter suggest it is important for women to meet together without men present?

3. What is sexism? How is it like a disease? A sin?

4. Why do women tend to introduce themselves in relation to their parents, husband, and/or children? What does that tendency say about a woman's own sense of completeness?

5. Do you see marriage as the union of two whole or two half-persons? What difference does it make?

## The Birth of the Shalom Woman

6. How is the entry into wholeness like a new birth? How is it risky, uncomfortable? How does it enable us to discover who we really are?

7. What is the importance of having to rely on one's own inner strength?

8. What are some old wineskins that you feel you may have to discard (p. 28)?

9. "The shalom woman must be prepared for a period of trial and rejection" (p. 28). Invite those in your group who have experienced such to share their pain and suffering.

10. How might we support each other in this new birth of wholeness?

## Walking as a Shalom Person

11. Notice that the author is not proposing that women conquer and subdue. Compare a life stance of "being and relating" with one of "conquering and subduing." What are some of the areas of life that would be affected? How is this contrary to our present culture?


## CHAPTER 3: HER THEOLOGY

1. What is symbolic about the Berlin Wall for women?

2. "Perhaps the greatest pain women bear from the church is being pushed to the periphery of the church's life and ministry" (p. 34). How has this occurred in your church body, in your congregation, in your own life?

3. Many in the women's movement see the church as being responsible for sanctifying and perpetuating the sin of sexism. In what ways is this an accurate analysis and how is it inaccurate? What is there in the Judeo-Christian tradition that is contrary to this analysis? What do we need to recover?

4. Do you think of yourself as a minister? As a theologian? If not, why not? What are some factors

preventing the entire human community from being taken seriously in the theologizing process? What might happen if the perspectives of all people were included?

## Woman and the Image of God

5. What do Jesus' "father" references to God imply? Is there anything inherently male about the God to whom he is so related?

6. If you try to conceive of God as feminine, how are your feelings different? Do you experience "her" to be closer than God as "him"? The author is not advocating switching all masculine references to feminine, but is asking us to realize how we have tended to absolutize the "maleness" of God.

## Women and the Incarnation

7. Discuss the crucial role of Mary in the incarnation.

## Women and the Ministry of Jesus

8. The author cites five ways in which Jesus responded to women. Discuss some of these attitudes of Jesus (pp. 40-45).

X
9. How has the church since ignored or contradicted Jesus' attitude to women?

10. Who were the first witnesses of the Resurrection?

11. How does Pentecost represent a "new day" for women (p. 47)?


# CHAPTER 4: HER CHURCH

1. The author challenged an old tradition in the Moravian church she attended. What are some traditions that you might challenge in your church in regard to church supper workers, council presidents, nursery helpers, ushers?

√
## The Traditional Biblical Record

2. What has happened to the prophetic voice given to women at Pentecost (p. 51)?

√
3. How is the social situation of women different from Paul's day? How does this affect his statements about women?

4. How has the story of the Fall affected the church's attitude toward sex and women?

5. Discuss some of the women mentioned in the Bible. Which one might be a viable model for you?

6. Compare the participation of women in your church body with that of the Evangelical Lutheran Church of Saxony.

7. Consider this possibility: Our pressure to force men into positions of top responsibility in the congregation may be one reason why they drop out of congregational activity.

## Women in Seminaries and in the Ordained Ministry

8. Talk to a woman who is ordained or in a seminary. What struggles does she face? How might you be supportive of her?

9. Many people seem to imply that ordaining women is the big hurdle. What hurdles follow?

## The Traditional Women's Auxiliaries

10. Is the description of the women's auxiliary typical of your church? How do you feel about its role and power?

11. How does the comparison between Lutheran men and women as described in A Study of Generations apply to your own congregation (pp. 67-68)?


## CHAPTER 5: HER RELATIONSHIPS

1. The shalom covenant allows freedom to exercise honest options in all relationships. It respects the individual and the common good. How do most of our relationships compare with it?

## Relationships with Men

2. How do our expectations for males and females contradict God's calling? What tragedies result?

3. The roles of women and men are complex in any culture. Contrast the Third World situation with that of women in more affluent cultures in regard to staying at home, childbearing, life expectancy, education, employment, etc.

4. What are some of the old cultural contracts that you would like to renegotiate (p. 81)? How can you go about changing them? How can we help the other person involved in a relationship to change also?

5. How is marriage changing among people you know? Which spouse is having the most difficulties adjusting?

6. How might the church be more helpful in relating to the changing concepts of marriage? What does your pastor think?

## Relationships with Children

7. How often have you heard the problems of children blamed on the mother? How often on the father? Is the working father as much to blame as the working mother?

8. The stereotype of masculine vs. feminine behavior says that males are active and thrusting, whereas females are passive and receptive. What does Dr. Hartlic[?] say about this (pp. 85-87)?

9. Polly and Jan talk about their experiences as young mothers. How did having children change your life? What were some of the happy and unhappy aspects? How might others, including the church, have helped?

10. Check out the child-related services provided in your community. What needs are not being met? How might your church help meet these needs?

11. "Shalom concerns itself with all children, everywhere" (p. 90). Examine your own attitudes toward the adoption of children of another race.

## Relationships with Other Women

12. Women have been conditioned to think about their relationship with men prior to their relationship with other women. Why? Discuss some of these factors: The value of relating to women; women's self-image; trusting other women; women's competition with each other; women being "their own worst enemy."

13. Our reaction against change causes us to justify our own position. Think of examples of this in your life and in the lives of those you know. Opposition to the Equal Rights Amendment is an example to consider.

14. "Shalom does not permit privileged women to take advantage of less privileged women" (p. 93). How is this sometimes violated?

15. How do you feel about the definition of partnership found on pp. 93-94? How might situations change if you were to apply it more fully in your relationship with other women, men, and children?


## CHAPTER 6: HER CONCERNS

1. What dangers are inherent in assuming that women' plight is due to any one political or economic system?

2. How does "shalom well-being" differ from the usua[l] American sense of "well-being"? What kind of global awareness is involved?

3. Read Olivia Nyembezi Mukuna's letter (pp. 102-03). What are the obvious difficulties in talking about liberation on the basis of such diverse experiences? Why is diversity essential?

## Women in the U.S.

4. The author describes the inadequate representation of women in the judicial and legal system. What disturbs you most about that? How are or could you be involved in helping to change that situation?

5. What is the usual reason given for paying women workers less? Why is that not accurate?

6. Investigate the salaries paid to men and women in jobs of comparable skill and responsibility in the place you or your spouse works, in church staff positions in your congregation or denomination, or in some other occupation or profession. What do the differences say about the value placed on work done by one sex or the other?

7. Think of the people you know who are separated or divorced. Do the author's observations regarding divorce apply to them (pp. 109-111)? If the couples are over 40, were the divorces instigated by the husband? How has the woman adjusted? How has the man?

8. Some people blame the rising divorce rate on the changing images and roles of women. Why is that an unfair analysis? Perhaps the church needs to take leadership in helping couples redefine themselves and their marriage. How might your church be involved?

9. What are some problems unique to the middle-aged or older woman who seeks to enter the job market? Are any groups in your area assisting women in making this move?

10. Why do married and divorced women often have difficulties relating to each other? Why is it important for them to acknowledge their feelings of fear or guilt? Try to encourage open, supportive ways for these two groups to share their feelings with each other.

11. Explain this statement found on p. 111: "The problems of the aged in the U.S. are largely a woman's problem." What is the predominant sex of the aged population in your congregation, local convalescent hospital, or in the general population in your community? How might women over 65 be helped to lead meaningful lives?

12. How might you as a "shalom woman" or man be an agent of change?

## CHAPTER 7: HER HOPES

Having looked at the past and present situations of women, it would be tempting to give up by exclaiming, "It's hopeless! Why bother with change?" However, the richness of the Christian faith means that in the face of discouragement, new hope emerges. Celebration bursts forth in the midst of and in spite of our differences. You might want to make this last session of your study a kind of celebration in which the group:

a) shares the pains and joys you have been experiencing through individual growth and your discoveries together;

b) affirms the growth and change (that is, celebrate, praise, and thank God and each other);

c) finds individual and corporate ways to express who you are, such as creating a symbol or ritual for your group or sharing in the Eucharist that makes us all one, etc.;

d) makes plans for moving on from here;

e) considers using the words of Mary Tulip as a covenant with each other (p. 122).

For additional resources and data, see the author's bibliography (p. 125) or contact:

    Church Women United, 475 Riverside, New York, N.Y. 10027

    Commission on the Status and Role of Women, United Methodist Church, 2121 N. Sheridan, Evanston, Ill. 60201

    Ecumenical Women's Centers, 1653 W. School St., Chicago, Ill. 60657

    Office of Women's Affairs of the Graduate Theological Union, 2465 LeConte Ave., Berkeley, Calif. 94709

    Women Committted to Women, 817 W. 34th St., Los Angeles, Calif. 90007

    Women's Center for Theologizing, 4051 Broadway, Kansas City, Mo. 64111

You might also want to communicate with:

    Task Force on Full Participation of Women in the Church, The American Lutheran Church, 422 S. Fifth St., Minneapolis, Minn. 55415

    Consulting Committee on Women in Church and Society, Lutheran Church in America, 231 Madison Ave., New York, N.Y. 10016